ALLEN CARR

with John Dicey

EASY WAY
TO QUIT

COCAINE

ALLEN CARR

with John Dicey

EASY WAY
TO QUIT
COCAINE

SIRIUS

SIRIUS

This edition published in 2022 by Sirius Publishing, a division of
Arcturus Publishing Limited,
26/27 Bickels Yard, 151–153 Bermondsey Street,
London SE1 3HA

ISBN: 978-1-3988-0886-7
AD010332US

Printed in the US

Allen Carr

Allen Carr was a chain-smoker for over 30 years. In 1983, after countless failed attempts to quit, he went from 60–100 cigarettes a day to zero without suffering withdrawal pangs, without using willpower, and without putting on weight. He realized that he had discovered what the world had been waiting for – the easy way to stop smoking – and embarked on a mission to help cure the world's smokers.

As a result of the phenomenal success of his method, he gained an international reputation as the world's leading expert on stopping smoking and his network of centers now spans the globe. His first book, Allen Carr's Easy Way to Stop Smoking, has sold over 17 million copies, remains a global bestseller, and has been published in more than 40 different languages. Hundreds of thousands of smokers have successfully quit at Allen Carr's Easyway centers where, with a success rate of over 90 per cent, it's guaranteed you'll find it easy to stop or your money back.

Allen Carr's brilliant Easyway method has been successfully applied to weight control, alcohol, debt, refined sugar, cannabis, cocaine, and a host of other addictions and issues.

For more information about Allen Carr's Easyway, please
visit **www.allencarr.com**

ALLEN CARR'S EASYWAY

The key that will set you free

CONTENTS

Introduction 9

Chapter 1 The Key 15

Chapter 2 A Positive Mindset 21

Chapter 3 The Trap 28

Chapter 4 Seeing Things As They Really Are 33

Chapter 5 Addiction 44

Chapter 6 Excuses 57

Chapter 7 Willpower 66

Chapter 8 Reconnect With Your Natural Faculties 73

Chapter 9 The Incredible Machine 86

Chapter 10 Getting Free 95

Chapter 11 Regaining Control 106

Chapter 12 Removing Fear 115

Chapter 13 First Steps to Freedom 121

Chapter 14 Ready to Quit 130

Chapter 15 Your Final Line 142

Chapter 16 Freedom Starts Here 147

Allen Carr's Easyway Centers 152

It is essential that you do not skip this important

Introduction

by John Dicey, Global CEO and Senior Therapist, Allen Carr's Easyway

Welcome to *Allen Carr's Easy Way to Quit Cocaine*. Allen Carr's reputation in the field of addiction treatment was built on his huge success in helping smokers quit. His Easyway method was so successful that it quickly became, and remains, a global phenomenon. From the earliest days of Easyway, Allen was inundated with requests from sufferers of countless other addictions and issues, imploring him to relate his method to their predicament. By the turn of the century, Allen had assembled a team of bright, loyal and dedicated senior therapists who went on to help him not only apply the method to all those addictions and issues, but also play a key role in delivering Allen Carr's Easyway method across the globe.

The responsibility for ensuring that our books are faithful to Allen Carr's original method is mine, and it's an honor to be writing this important introduction. Rest assured, once you've read it, I'll leave you in Allen's capable hands. It has been suggested to me that I describe myself as the author of the books we've published since Allen passed away. In my view, that would be quite wrong.

That's because every new book is written strictly in accordance with Allen Carr's brilliant Easyway method. In our new books, we have just updated the content, context, and format to make them as relevant as possible for the modern-day audience, while also incorporating upgraded elements of the method developed during the tens of thousands of hours spent treating addicts of all kinds at our live seminars. There is not a word in our books that Allen didn't write or wouldn't have written if he were still with us and, for that reason, the updates, anecdotes and analogies that are not his own work—that were modernized or added by me—are written clearly in Allen's voice to seamlessly complement the original text and method.

I consider myself privileged to have worked very closely with Allen on Easyway books while he was still alive, getting insight into how the method could be applied, and we explored and mapped out its future evolution together. I was more than happy to have the responsibility of continuing this vital mission placed on my shoulders by Allen himself. It's a responsibility I accepted with humility and one I take extremely seriously.

WHAT ARE OUR CREDENTIALS?

We've been treating addicts all over the world with phenomenal success over the past 35 years. The senior members of my team and I were inspired to join Allen's quest for one simple reason: his method saved our lives. Like every Allen Carr's Easyway Therapist in the world, we were drawn to Easyway as a result of being set free of our own addictions.

It was a pleasure to work with Allen in assembling the most remarkable senior therapist team to undertake the task of applying the method to issues other than smoking, so that it could help people escape from the misery of alcohol addiction, weight issues, sugar addiction, as well as cocaine, marijuana and opioid addiction and a host of other addictions and issues.

The drug-taking history of Allen's senior therapist team, far from deterring Allen and myself from recruiting them, encouraged us to do so. If Allen was impressed by your drive, enthusiasm, ability and accomplishments, he considered it a superb bonus if you had previously experienced the misery of other addictions. He was acutely aware that it would be extremely difficult to apply his method to the full range of addictions without the direct involvement of people who had used the method to set themselves free of those drugs. Whether it be heroin, cocaine, marijuana, alcohol, nicotine, serious weight issues or sugar addiction, direct, up close and personal experience of those drugs and issues enabled Allen and his team to develop the method accordingly.

This book is the direct result of our experience in treating cocaine addicts for more than 20 years at Allen Carr's flagship center in London. Addicts have flown in from every corner of the globe to seek our help. So you can rest reassured, this program is tried and tested, and is effective regardless of your nationality or location. When we started treating cocaine addiction, we were so confident in the program we had created that we even provided the same money-back guarantee for cocaine addicts that we had been providing to smokers since the inception of the method. If they didn't quit the drug, we refunded their fee in full.

The treatment is expensive—for cocaine and other drugs, the live seminars are delivered on a one-on-one basis, as opposed to our other seminars, which are normally delivered in groups of 20 to 25 people—so, naturally, we had to charge more. But we were determined to ensure that people buying the service could do so with absolute confidence. If they completed the program and failed to quit the drug, their fee was refunded in full.

Over the last 20 years, in spite of the relative expense of the live one-on-one cocaine seminars, the refund rate has been less than 5 per cent, and we continue to offer the money-back guarantee to this day (and the live seminars delivered via Zoom are equally effective). There are a whole host of expensive rehab treatment centers around the world. But we remain, to our knowledge, the only provider of addiction services that provides any form of money-back guarantee. How can we do that?

SIMPLE: THIS METHOD WORKS!

Our motivation for putting the method down in writing and into an Online Video Program was to enable anyone, anywhere in the world, regardless of their level of wealth, to benefit from *Allen Carr's Easy Way to Quit Cocaine*.

This book isn't simply a transcript of our live one-on-one seminars—those are dynamic, interactive, last six hours, and include telephone/email support and free-of-charge backup sessions—but, like our Online Video Program, it is certainly the next best thing.

Make no mistake, this book is a complete program in itself, so please don't be put off by the mention of the live seminars or the online video program. You have in your hands the most up-to-date, cutting-edge version of Allen Carr's Easyway to Quit Cocaine method—and this book will set you free.

I'm aware that many people who are unfamiliar with the method, or who have never met people who have successfully quit with Easyway, assume that some of the claims made about it are far-fetched or exaggerated. That was certainly my reaction when I first heard them. I was incredibly fortunate to have had my life saved by Allen Carr. There is no doubt that, had I not come into contact with Allen and his amazing method, more than a little reluctantly I should add, in the late 1990s, I wouldn't have made it to the 21st century. I was so inspired by my newfound freedom, I couldn't wait to offer Allen my assistance to help him achieve his goals.

I'm incredibly proud to have headed up the team that, over the last 23 years, has taken Allen's method from Berlin to Brasília, from New Zealand to New York, from Sydney to Santiago and beyond.

I still take pleasure in deflecting all the praise and acclaim straight back to the great man himself: it's all thanks to Allen Carr.

The method is as pure, as bright, as adaptable, and as effective as it's ever been, allowing us to apply it to a whole host of addictions and issues. Whether it's cocaine, heroin, alcohol or sugar addiction, gambling or debt, fear of flying, mindfulness, or even digital/social media addiction, the method guides those who need help in a simple, relatable, plain-speaking way.

Please don't mistake Allen Carr's Easyway method for some kind of Jack of all trades. As you're about to discover for yourself, there is no doubt that it truly is the master of all addictions.

Now, without further delay, let me pass you into the safest of hands—Allen Carr and his Easyway.

Chapter 1

THE KEY

This book will give you all the information you need to set yourself free of cocaine. More importantly, you will stay free, and you will find it ridiculously easy. That's the whole point of Easyway.

At this stage you probably find that a little hard to believe, but don't worry about that. Skepticism is a good thing. In fact, it's a great tool, and you'll be required to use it throughout this book. I want you to be skeptical not just about everything I say, but about everything you've been led to believe about cocaine.

You might be surprised to learn that virtually everything you think you know about cocaine is actually the opposite of the truth. Hold that thought. We'll return to it later.

A METHOD THAT WORKS

You'll be glad to learn that the method you are going to use to set yourself free has done the same for millions of people around the world. I discovered it when I finally succeeded in quitting smoking after more than 30 years of chain-smoking 60 to 100 cigarettes a day.

I had tried all the conventional methods to quit, and unconventional ones too, all kinds of substitutes and gimmicks. But nothing worked.

It was like being between the devil and the deep blue sea. I desperately wanted to quit, but whenever I tried I was utterly miserable. No matter how long I survived, I never felt completely free—it was as if I'd lost my best friend, my crutch, my character, my very personality.

In those days, I really believed that there were such types as addictive personalities, or that there was something in our genes that meant we couldn't enjoy life or cope with stress without the drug.

Maybe that resonates with you.

Eventually, after countless failed attempts to quit, I gave up on trying to stop, and resigned myself to a lifetime of slavery. Then I discovered something that motivated me to try again. *I went overnight from 100 cigarettes a day to zero, without any bad temper or sense of loss, void, or depression. On the contrary, I actually enjoyed the process.*

It didn't take me long to realize that I had discovered a method that could enable any smoker to quit easily, immediately, without feeling deprived, without using willpower, substitutes, or other gimmicks, without suffering depression or unpleasant withdrawal symptoms, and without gaining weight.

After trying out the method on smoking friends and relatives with great success, I gave up my successful career in the financial world to devote myself to helping other smokers quit. I called the method Easyway, and it has become a global success story, with Easyway centers now in over 150 cities in more than 50 countries worldwide.

Bestselling books based on my method are now translated into more than 40 languages, with more being added each year.

So what does this have to do with your cocaine addiction?

It quickly dawned on me that if the method worked so well for nicotine, it could just as easily be applied to any drug addiction. And it's true. Easyway has helped tens of millions of people quit smoking, alcohol, cocaine, cannabis, opioids, sugar addiction and achieve freedom from weight issues, even junk-spending, caffeine addiction, fear of flying, and even tech addiction for those who have issues with smartphones, gaming and digital overload.

Make no mistake, this isn't a case of Easyway being a Jack of all trades. It is the master of all addictions. Including cocaine.

SO WHAT'S THE SECRET?
There's no secret. The method works by removing the sense of deprivation that addicts suffer from when they try to quit with other methods. It removes the feeling that you are making a sacrifice. Unlike other methods you might have tried, it doesn't rely on willpower.

That might all sound too good to be true, but rest assured, all you have to do is read this book all the way to the end, follow all the instructions, and you will be set free of your addiction to cocaine.

Perhaps you're not even sure you are addicted to cocaine; maybe you just need a little help to get things into perspective, to cut down on the impact it's having on your life. The fact is, it doesn't matter whether you consider yourself an addict, or someone who just has a little too much, a little too often. Just follow this method, and it will work for you.

Whatever form of cocaine or crack you take; regardless of whether you snort it, smoke it, inject it or take it by any other means; whether you mix it with booze, MDMA, ket, weed, anything else or some or all of the above, this program will set you free.

"IS IT GONNA SNOW TONIGHT?"
Nicknames and slang for coke have evolved over the years. There are hundreds of different names around the world. Whatever you call it, we'll just keep it simple here and refer to it generically as cocaine or coke.

NO NEED FOR WILLPOWER
Most coke addicts are convinced that it's difficult to quit. The problem, we're told, is not only the physical withdrawal but also that we have

to use willpower to resist the craving. The great news is that you don't have to use willpower, suffer bad withdrawal pangs, or use substitutes. And you don't have to feel deprived or be left with a huge feeling of sacrifice.

If you've tried to quit cocaine in the past and failed, if you've battled feelings of deprivation and sacrifice and ended up eventually succumbing to temptation, please put those experiences behind you. This method is different.

We're going to address the task from an entirely different angle. Other methods go on and on about the downsides of coke addiction: the physical harm, the cost, the slavery, the shame, the low self-esteem, the feelings of hopelessness, feelings of weakness, the feeling that you aren't "you" any more, the destruction of relationships, or the self-disgust.

That's not part of Easyway. It's patronizing and pointless.

If those factors were ever going to help you break free of coke addiction, they would have done so by now and you wouldn't be reading this book. Every cocaine addict knows all about the downsides, and it doesn't help them get free.

Rather than use the downsides in an attempt to motivate yourself to freedom, set them aside. Once you're free, release from those factors will simply be a wonderful bonus.

Instead, think about this question:

WHAT'S SO GREAT ABOUT BEING A COKE ADDICT?

We'll return to it later.

For now, rest assured, you're on a well-trodden path. More than 50 million people have used Easyway already. They didn't come across the method as a result of multimillion-dollar marketing and advertising campaigns; they came across it as the result of the oldest and most reliable means of referral: word of mouth.

The best ad for Easyway is all the people who have used it to quit. Thirty years ago, it was a slightly slower, more cumbersome process. Someone would try the method, be freed of their addiction, and tell their family, friends and colleagues about their success. Their family, friends and colleagues saw the evidence with their own eyes.

These former addicts weren't suffering, they weren't hiding away, fearful that they might fall back into the addiction. They appeared to be enjoying life, handling stress, relaxing, socializing and having fun, coping with the ups and downs of life without showing the slightest interest in taking the drug again. It didn't matter whether it was nicotine, alcohol, cocaine, sugar or any other drug; the effect was the same:

FREEDOM.

WHY YOU'RE READING THIS BOOK

It was literally word of mouth that carried news of Easyway across the globe in those early days, well before the birth of the internet, social media and digital marketing. It became a global phenomenon at breakneck speed, the old-fashioned way.

Of course, more recently word of mouth has become even speedier and more effective. With social media, bloggers and instant communication, good news travels faster than ever.

In fact, it's likely that the reason you're reading this book, the means by which you originally discovered this method, was via a member of your family, a friend, or a colleague telling you about their own success with it.

Now it's your turn. Get ready to break free of cocaine.

Let this be the first day of an exciting adventure; the day you start preparing yourself to be free. All you need to do is follow the instructions.

In fact, your first instruction is:

FOLLOW ALL THE INSTRUCTIONS.

You could spend a lifetime trying to break into a safe and still not succeed. But if you know the correct combination to the lock, or if you have the key, it's ridiculously easy. Skip just one number in the combination, or lose the key, and the safe that holds your freedom stays locked.

This book contains the key—the combination of information you need in order to become free. It will enable you to escape from cocaine addiction. Follow the instructions and you will succeed. Ignore one of them and you jeopardize your entire objective.

Your second instruction is:

DON'T ATTEMPT TO CUT DOWN.

It's important that you not try to control your cocaine use until you are advised to do so. That will be toward the end of this book.

Of course, if you have already abstained for a few days, there is no need to resume taking it. But if you currently use cocaine and decide to read this book over the next two days, and tonight you're out and want to use coke, do so. I don't want you to use willpower to resist your coke craving, because that would interfere with this program. But be sure to only read this book when you are not under the influence of any drug, including alcohol.

Chapter 2

A POSITIVE MINDSET

To find it easy to quit cocaine, you must achieve a state of mind whereby whenever you think about coke you feel a sense of release, freedom and relief that you don't consume it anymore. That really is the only way to become and remain truly free, and no longer vulnerable to the drug.

Changing—or, more accurately, correcting—your perception of cocaine will be an exciting, eye-opening and positive experience and, although you might find that hard to believe, you have absolutely nothing to lose and everything to gain by accepting that it's going to be exactly that way.

Your third instruction is:

START OFF IN A HAPPY FRAME OF MIND.

Closely followed by the fourth instruction:

THINK POSITIVELY.

Set aside all feelings of impending doom and gloom. Nothing bad is going to happen, and there is no need to be miserable or anticipate failure or difficulty. You're about to achieve something truly wonderful, something amazing.

See your short journey to freedom for what it really is: an exciting challenge, an adventure. Just think of how proud you'll feel when you're free. This might be a private achievement for you—something that will remain a secret from those who are nearest and dearest to you. But don't let that temper the feeling of pride. You're about to impress the most important person on the planet:

YOU!

The fifth instruction is the most difficult to follow:

KEEP AN OPEN MIND.

The importance of this cannot be overemphasized. Some people believe that Easyway is a form of brainwashing. In a way, that's a tribute to its effectiveness; but the fact is, nothing could be further from the truth. What this method actually does is:

COUNTER-BRAINWASHING.

If you imagine brainwashing as the gradual over-tightening of a coil or spring, what Easyway does, over the course of reading this book, is gradually, painlessly and safely stop the unnatural and damaging over-tightening process, and then gently and calmly reverse it—eventually leaving the coil or spring in its natural, healthy, safe condition.

That is counter-brainwashing.

This method involves the reversal of false beliefs that you might have had your entire life. You need to question what you think you know about cocaine. Question what society, other addicts and even your own experiences have led you to believe about the drug. If you can do that, and you follow all the other instructions, you cannot fail.

Take a look at these different-sized coffee cups.

If I were to tell you that they're all the same size, you'd be extremely skeptical, wouldn't you? You've already accepted that they're different sizes because that's what I told you, and it aligns with what you see.

Nevertheless, the fact is, they are all exactly the same size.

Look again. Still skeptical? Take a ruler and measure them. Surprising, isn't it?

The reason for showing you this illusion is to demonstrate how the mind can easily be tricked into accepting something as true when, in fact, it's entirely false.

Your only frame of reference regarding cocaine is your addicted state of mind and body. In that context, a line of coke does seem to deliver a boost. In reality, though, it's dragging you down mentally and physically.

WHO'S IN CONTROL?

Do you think you use cocaine by choice? That might be the natural assumption. After all, you're the one who buys it, and you're the one who administers it to your body. But are you really acting out of free will?

If a friend appeared to get good returns on an investment, you might be tempted to join them and invest yourself. If it turned out that the investment was a con or a hustle that resulted in you and your friend losing all your money, would you regard that loss as being incurred through having made a genuine choice?

The fact is, you originally invested in the plan based on false information. You continued to invest based on the same. You didn't choose to lose your money—you were conned. This is a crucial point. It's not that you made a poor investment; that's simply part of the risk involved in such ventures. The fact is, you never stood a chance. It was a con. A rip-off.

Your cocaine use is the result of a similar confidence trick. Sure, you made the decision to start using it, but that decision was based on flawed information. You continued to use it based on the same misinformation, combined with the addiction.

Of course, you chose to have those first experimental lines, but how long ago was that? Years ago? Perhaps you were at an entirely different stage in your life. You were excited. It felt illicit. It felt sophisticated. It felt dangerous. But at no point in those early days did you make a decision to end up in your current predicament: to be dragged down so low by the drug that you had to seek professional help to stop taking it.

You're not reading this book because coke has become a slight inconvenience to you, nor because it occurred to you that it might be nice to stop using it. You chose to read this book because at some point, perhaps some time ago, you suddenly realized:

YOU'RE TRAPPED.

Yes, you decided to use cocaine when you started out. But at some imperceptible stage you realized that the reverse had become true. Coke was using you.

Deep down inside, you actually knew this fairly early on, but you brushed the thought aside. After all, you were convinced that you could take it or leave it—or at least that if you really wanted to stop using it, you could.

At what point did you decide you would need to use cocaine several times a month. Or every week? Or more days than not? Or even every day? At what point did you decide that, even if you didn't take it every day, you would end up bingeing on it—sometimes for days in a row, never being allowed to stop, just delaying and holding out for as long as possible until the next time and the next time and the next time?

The fact is, you didn't decide to become a cocaine addict and you didn't decide that you would need to use coke for the rest of your life. The simple truth is:

YOU DON'T CONTROL THE DRUG—THE DRUG CONTROLS YOU.

You know it controls you. And you know what it has cost you, not just in terms of money. You no longer use cocaine because it feels exciting. In fact, you're probably bored of it. You no longer use cocaine because it feels sophisticated. In fact, it makes you feel anything but sophisticated, doesn't it? And you don't use cocaine because it's illicit or dangerous. You use it in spite of that.

WHY YOU WANT TO QUIT

Clients who attend our one-on-one live seminars for cocaine—whether they do so in London, New York, LA, Miami, Bahrain, Singapore or Australia—give a variety of reasons why they want to quit:

"I want to feel in control again."

"I'm scared of losing my partner… my family… my job."

"I've finally acknowledged that I've got a problem."

"I'm addicted."

"I'm worried about the money and the things that coke makes me do, e.g. gambling."

"It's causing health problems."

"It's the paranoia."

"It's disgusting—I know I'm a better person than this."

"Life is getting bad—no emotions—it's changing me as a person."

"It's destroying my relationships."

"Everything has gone: my wife, my kids, my everything."

"The effect it's having on my body—and on my mind."

"It's ruining my social relationships."

"It makes me put myself in dangerous situations."

"Health, money, family."

"It forces me to be with people and do things with people I don't even like."

"It has taken over my life and ruined my relationships—and I've finally had enough."

"I'm out of control and it's affecting my work… I have two young children."

"It's taking over my life, making me depressed, and making me paranoid."

How many of those factors do you relate to? At least some; perhaps even all of them, as well as some others that I haven't even mentioned.

If you're remotely resistant to the idea that you no longer use cocaine out of choice, you need to ask yourself why on earth you're reading this book. If you are in control of your choice, exercising free will, why not just choose not to take it any more?

But it's not quite as simple as that, is it? And why isn't it that simple? Because you're a cocaine addict.

CUTTING DOWN

How many times have you tried to quit coke? Or cut down? And what happens? You might last a few days, or a week, or a month, or even more, but eventually you get sucked back in. And when that happens… it always seems harder to resist, doesn't it? You want it more frequently, earlier in the week, earlier in the day. More.

Cutting down and trying to control your intake of a drug to which you're addicted doesn't work, despite what other so-called experts might say. Telling someone to limit their intake of an addictive drug is like telling them they can jump off a building, as long as they don't fall more than a few feet. The force of addiction—just like the force of gravity—will always pull you down.

Later in the book we will look at why, with your previous attempts to quit, you might have fallen back into the trap from which you were trying to escape. More importantly, you will understand why it will be different this time, and you'll not only get free but stay free.

Having acknowledged that the reason you use cocaine isn't because you want to, or choose to, but simply because you're addicted to it, I have some great news for you. The addiction is actually easy to break. Just as long as you know how…

Chapter 3

THE TRAP

We'll talk about the high, the buzz, or the benefits you think you get from using cocaine in a while. First you need to understand how you become and remain addicted.

It can be frightening to admit that you're addicted to a drug, especially one with the reputation that cocaine has. But thankfully, the addiction is easy to break once you understand it.

Cocaine is a physically addictive drug, which means that after you consume it, it creates physical withdrawal, which takes the form of a mild, empty, slightly insecure, slightly uptight feeling. It's so mild, it's almost imperceptible.

When you take another dose of the drug, that mild, empty, insecure feeling temporarily disappears, leaving you feeling normal again. In fact, you use each dose of cocaine merely to try to return to the feeling you had all the time before you became addicted. That said, it's such a gradual process, you're not even aware that it's happening.

It's as if there's a little monster inside your body that feeds on cocaine. If you don't feed it, it complains. Feed it and the complaining stops for a while, only to return as the body withdraws again from the latest dose. When you break free of coke addiction, you're going to starve that Little Monster to death.

The physical withdrawal is very slight, remember. You go days, sometimes even weeks, without responding to it. Getting rid of the Little Monster is no more difficult than living with those almost imperceptible complaints for a short time. That's easy, as long as you're in the right frame of mind and follow some simple instructions. What makes quitting difficult is not the physical withdrawal itself but the fact that it acts as a trigger for the real problem:

THE BIG MONSTER.

The Little Monster in the body is related to a Big Monster in the brain. The Big Monster is created by brainwashing. We're brainwashed into believing that we get some kind of benefit or crutch from cocaine: that it helps us focus, or concentrate, that it dramatically increases our energy levels and helps us socialize. The effect of the Little Monster seems to confirm this.

When you use cocaine, that empty, insecure, slightly uptight feeling that cocaine created disappears for a while and you do feel less empty, less insecure and less uptight than you did a moment before. Withdrawal makes us feel physically lethargic but mentally restless. It's distracting and, therefore, impairs concentration. Each dose of cocaine seems to relieve these symptoms, and we are fooled into believing that this feeling of relief is a genuine pleasure or crutch.

It's this belief that creates the feeling of deprivation when we try to quit. And it's this feeling of deprivation that creates the cravings associated with cocaine withdrawal.

Remember, the physical withdrawal (the Little Monster) is very mild. It's the thought process that it triggers, aided and abetted by the brainwashing (the Big Monster), that causes the unpleasant cravings.

This method takes the Big Monster out of the equation. All you have to do then is starve the Little Monster to death by quitting cocaine, and you will be free. It sounds easy, doesn't it? The great news is that it is easy... when you know how.

THE PITCHER PLANT

The process of addiction is so slight, we're not even aware of it. It's a subtle process that traps its victims in the same way as a pitcher plant. Have you ever seen a pitcher plant?

This carnivorous plant is shaped like a pitcher, with a tall, jug-like body that opens up to a wider rim. The scent of its nectar attracts flies, which land on the rim and sip the nectar. As it sips, it is gradually lured further into the pitcher, but the slope at the top is so slight that the fly doesn't realize. By the time the slope has become steeper, the fly is too preoccupied with the nectar to notice.

When the fly gets just beyond the neck of the vase, it can see many dead insects in a pool of liquid at the bottom. But that doesn't bother it, because it knows it can fly away whenever it likes. So it feels safe continuing to gorge on the nectar. But by the time it's had enough, and decides to fly away, it finds that it can't. It's too far in. The nectar is sticking to its legs.

The fly panics and begins to struggle. The more it struggles to escape, the more it covers itself in the sticky nectar, which weighs it down even more and makes it impossible for it to get a grip on the sides of the plant, which are now vertical.

Pretty soon, the fly is joining the other dead insects in the liquid at the bottom of the pitcher, which is not nectar but the digestive juice of the plant.

When would you say the fly lost control?

Was it when it slid into the digestive juice? Was it when it tried to escape and found it couldn't? No, that was when it realized it had lost control, so it must have been before then.

Was it when it saw all the dead insects at the bottom of the plant then? Or was it somewhere on the gradual slope at the top?

Many people will say that the fly was in control at both of those stages, because it could have escaped if it had wanted to. But it didn't want to because it didn't realize it was in a trap.

So when did the fly lose control?

Was it when it first landed on the lip of the plant? No, it was even before that.

THE FLY WAS NEVER IN CONTROL.

It was subtly being controlled by the plant from the moment it got a whiff of the nectar.

That perfectly describes how cocaine hooks us without us even realizing it. The whiff of nectar is the brainwashing—the reputation and perceived advantages of cocaine use, which is all around us. In movies and books, among our friends and colleagues who used it, well before we even tried it, we were being lured by misinformation. As soon as we tried it, it seemed to confirm the brainwashing. And that's the point where we lost control.

Of course coke addicts, in fact any addicts, realize they're not in control quite early on, but we push it to the back of our minds, thinking we could easily escape if we wanted to.

The good news is that, unlike the fly, you are not standing on a slippery slope; there is no physical force compelling you to take more cocaine. The trap is entirely in your mind.

The fact that you are your own jailer is an ingenious aspect of the trap and, fortunately for you, it's also its fatal flaw. You have the power to escape simply by understanding the nature of the trap and following the easy instructions in this book.

COCAINE IS CONNING YOU

When you see the trap in these terms, the solution looks simple: stop using coke and just fly away. But as you know, when you're actually in the trap, nothing looks simple. That's because there are two major illusions corrupting your judgment:

1. The myth that cocaine gives you pleasure and some kind of benefit
2. The myth that escape will be hard and painful

We'll talk more about the illusion of pleasure and benefit a little later but, in short, the reason why we believe escape will be hard and painful is that we have been convinced that cocaine gives us some form of pleasure and benefit; therefore, stopping would mean making a sacrifice.

When you read stories about the suffering and pain celebrities have been through when trying to get clean—the repeated visits to rehab, the daily battle to stay clean—it's enough to keep you from even trying to quit. That's all part of the brainwashing.

Quitting IS painful if you go about it the hard way—using willpower—but this method is different.

It's time to unravel the illusions that have been keeping you in the cocaine trap.

Chapter 4

SEEING THINGS AS THEY REALLY ARE

Cocaine used to be seen as the drug of the rich and famous. That still rings true to an extent but, over the years, as the drug has become relatively less expensive and easier to obtain, cocaine addiction has become far more "inclusive."

The people we see at our specialist centers in London and all over the world via our live online one-on-one seminars now come from all walks of life. In most of the Western world, cocaine use is rampant, almost at epidemic levels.

Yes, we get CEOs of international companies, rock stars and movie stars, stock brokers and city slickers, but we also get stay-at-home moms, carpenters, gardeners, salespeople, personal assistants, hair stylists, chefs and waiters. We now see people from every imaginable walk of life.

Coke no longer cares whether you're rich, not so rich, or barely making ends meet.

But by picking up this book, you've done an amazing thing. You've ensured your freedom. You've made the decision that you're done with it.

You're about to escape from a miserable prison, and that's a wonderful thing.

It's time to stop being so hard on yourself. There is no reason or benefit in beating yourself up about what it's done to you and to those you love. Instead, feel great about getting free. You didn't do anything wrong, you just fell into an ingenious trap—the same trap that has snared millions of other people. By the end of this book, you will realize the truth.

You were conned. Ignore the downsides of the drug. Let's be clear about this: no one has ever gotten free of addiction by focusing on the disadvantages of the drug.

SO, WHAT ARE THE BENEFITS OF COCAINE?

When people attend our cocaine seminars we ask them, "What benefits do you think you get from cocaine?"

It comes back to the reasons why we first started using cocaine: to be edgy, to appear sophisticated or wild, to rebel or, the opposite, to fit in with our peer group. There's a whole host of foolish reasons why we started experimenting with the drug, and in your current predicament they probably seem childish and naïve. Just remember, intelligent people fall for confidence tricks. You didn't make a bad investment or even a bad decision. You were conned.

You tried cocaine and it seemed to live up to its publicity:

1. It seemed to act as a stimulant and help you party harder for longer, drink more alcohol for longer, or work harder for longer.
2. It appeared to provide some kind of escape, to help you block out life, block out problems, get rid of worries, and ease depression.
3. It seemed like fun, and it seemed to help you lose your inhibitions.
4. You felt high, buzzed, excited, and exciting.

5. It seemed to give you confidence and make you feel interesting and even invincible.
6. It seemed to become a habit.

The fact is that you had already been brainwashed into believing that cocaine could do all those things for you. TV dramas, Hollywood movies, rock stars and pretty much everyone you had ever seen taking the drug or talking about the drug seemed to be a walking, talking advertisement for it. You were primed to expect certain things from the drug.

As you now know, all was not as it seemed. In the early days, though, that's harder to see.

Someone who attended one of our coke seminars was beautifully honest about his beliefs about what cocaine did for him.

"On one hand," he said, "it makes me feel like I'm a better person, that everything is possible, that I can write better lyrics for my songs, that I can talk to girls more easily and effectively."

He made it sound like the perfect drug! Then he said, "Deep in my heart, though, I know it made me a crushing bore spouting nonsense. I never wrote good lyrics after I'd taken it, and it was never easier for me to get to know girls. I was kidding myself."

Another attendee was also brutally honest. "I'm a nice guy; that's my nature. I love being a nice guy—people like me. But add booze or coke—or, more often than not, both—and what do you get? An instant a**hole."

His words, not mine.

The rock-star lifestyle or image is an amazing mind trick. Take your pick of generations: for my generation, the ultimate icon would have been someone like David Bowie—just about the coolest, most "out-there" artist on the planet during the 1970s, 80s and beyond.

Do a YouTube search for "David Bowie" and "cocaine." You'll find several interviews from the early 70s, when he was clearly under the influence of coke (among other drugs). He doesn't look cool or glamorous or rebellious or hedonistic; he looks like a mere shadow of himself, a fidgety, twitching, nervous wreck. His brilliance still shines through, but he looks half dead, pathetic, embarrassing, and awkward as he constantly makes weird, distorted faces.

There's nothing there that would ever truly generate admiration—not really. Sadly, some would find it funny, or feel he was an example of someone living life on the edge, but what do you really see? It is here that you see cocaine for exactly what it is. Sucking the life, talent and spirit out of truly gifted and great people.

In case you think I'm missing the point, and that Bowie had a happy relationship with cocaine and used it to fuel his genius, this is what he said when reflecting on why he stopped taking it. "You can't have relationships with anybody—you don't let anyone else exist—you just become a really dreadful person, and I just think I got fed up with being a really dreadful person."

Does that ring a bell?

Now let's look at the other perceived benefits of using cocaine.

THE BUZZ

It is true that cocaine is a powerful stimulant, and most people are now aware that powerful stimulants cause huge problems rather than solve them.

First of all, you are perfectly equipped to live your life without phony stimulants. Look at children running around at a party with apparently endless energy and excitement. They're on a completely natural energy high, a completely natural emotional high—and that's

BEFORE they're force-fed chemical- and sugar-laden candy, cake, and ice cream.

As kids, we don't need sugar or caffeine or cocaine for energy boosts; put a bunch of kids in a park with a ball and leave them for a few hours, and they'll play virtually non-stop. They might pause for a drink from time to time, but that's it. In most cases they'll play until it's too dark to play any more.

They're on a completely natural high, and their bodies are perfectly equipped to perform at those extraordinary levels. You were like that once. In fact, you still are. You just need to treat your body right.

Even as adults, our natural state should be feeling energized. As long as you're not sick, you should have more than enough energy to do whatever you want to do in life.

If you're really tired, your body is asking for sleep and rest. It's certainly not asking for cocaine!

Using coke is like taking out a payday loan; after a quick injection of cash (energy), they've got you hooked, with interest, for the rest of your life, and you have to go back for more and more, again and again, until you make your mind up to do something about it.

The reality is that coke addiction makes you permanently tired and exhausted.

It often leads you to overload on caffeine, too, which is like pouring gasoline on a fire. Take a look at anyone with a caffeine or coke problem—or a caffeine *and* coke problem. They look tired, run down, lethargic and ready to drop. The irony is, the only thing preventing them from returning to their energetic, athletic, vivacious former self is the very thing they think is helping them: coffee and cocaine.

But what about those times when you need a little pick-me-up to get through a late shift, or keep you going until the end of a long day?

Well, there are many natural, harmless, non-addictive and healthy stimulants that can help you.

How do non-coke addicts get through life? They get home from work; it's been a long, hard week and they're committed to going out. They really wanted to go, but they're feeling tired, and not so excited about it. They don't want to let their partner or friends down by canceling, so they freshen up, maybe take a shower, get changed and emerge for their night out, excited and not remotely tired. They're buzzing for a night out now.

Coke addicts can experience that natural energy regeneration too—but they credit it to cocaine.

To use cocaine to get you ready for a big night out, or to enable you to keep drinking for longer, is one of the biggest contradictions. Alcohol is a depressant and cocaine is a stimulant—the combination is counterproductive. In fact, in the cold light of day, when you listen to someone addicted to cocaine talk about the relationship between cocaine and alcohol, it highlights exactly how pointless the poisonous cycle is. When other drugs are involved, it becomes even more so.

Far from being a cure for tiredness, cocaine leaves you exhausted, taking another line of coke just to get out of bed and a few lines just to get in the mood to go out.

COKE DESTROYS YOUR ENERGY!

Perhaps you fear that you'll have to quit alcohol too once you're free of cocaine. That would only be the case if you used the willpower method. When you use willpower to battle an addiction, you always have to resist the temptation to take the drug. After a few drinks, that resistance is worn away and you cave in. But with this method, you eliminate the temptation, so there is no need or desire to take the drug, no matter how much alcohol you might consume.

A TUG-OF-WAR

There are so many disadvantages to using cocaine, but there is nothing to gain in focusing on those. You know all about them already: the money, the insomnia, the fatigue, the nightmares, the paranoia, the low self-esteem and shame. This knowledge hasn't stopped you before and it won't stop you now.

The fact that so much street coke is cut with baking soda, Novocaine, speed, and things that are probably even more poisonous than the coke doesn't seem to bother us. Neither does the appalling way it makes us treat people around us, be they loved ones or just innocent bystanders unfortunate enough to stumble across us when we're on it.

We know all the downsides, but we kid ourselves that there's some sort of payoff, some positive aspect to the drug that outweighs and blocks our minds to all the downsides. So we have this tug-of-war going on between two conflicting fears: on one side the fear of what it's doing to us; on the other side the fear of what life would be like without the drug and the advantages we think it gives us.

Whichever way we look at the situation, we feel fear. And it's fear that keeps us hooked.

The fear at both ends of that tug-of-war is caused by one thing: cocaine.

MYTHS

What is it that coke addicts worry about losing or missing out on if they quit? There's the one about booze and coke—the belief that if you do coke you can drink more, because one drug cancels out the effect of the other. That's a weird struggle to feel normal. You could achieve the very same effect by not taking either drug in the first place!

Keith (not his real name) was a client on one of our one-on-one online live seminars recently. He was in New York and our therapist was in London.

Keith had clearly had an extremely privileged upbringing. He'd never had to work, not in the sense that you or I might consider it, and had never had any real responsibility. He had a pretty much limitless supply of cash. The kind of checks on addiction that most people have just weren't there. He never had to get up for work in the morning, he always had someone cleaning up after him, and he had no money worries at all.

He explained that he would come to in the morning so wrecked from the previous night's activities that he'd do three or four really fat lines just to get out of bed. He'd always do too much, so then he'd take some heroin to bring himself down off the coke. But he'd always do too much of that, too.

He'd want to drive to lunch, so he'd do some more coke to bring himself up again and, of course, at lunch he'd have plenty of booze. So much booze, in fact, that he'd be too drunk to drive—so he'd do some more coke to help him "straighten out" enough to do that. Straighten out enough in *his* view, that is. All day long Keith would do coke to negate the effects of booze and heroin, and heroin and booze to negate the effects of coke.

All he was trying to do was feel normal.

That notion was like a revelation to him. It never occurred to him that he could get exactly the same effect by just drinking less and not taking the drugs in the first place. It's the partying harder for longer that usually brings coke addicts to the point where they realize they can't keep taking the drug. It's when you override your body's warning mechanisms that real problems occur.

Tiredness isn't a weakness. It's your body telling you that you need to rest. Becoming sluggish when you've had too much to drink is your body telling you that you're poisoning yourself and need to stop. You override those warning mechanisms at your peril.

NOTHING TO GIVE UP

Quitting coke doesn't mean giving up partying. In fact, you'll enjoy parties more and you'll be better company once you've quit. You'll also keep better company.

A few months after attending his seminar and getting off cocaine, Keith dropped us a line. He said, "Far from becoming a hermit or living like a monk, I've been partying harder than ever! More energy, more fun, more everything—all without the coke. Even better, I realized that I didn't even like some of the people I'd hang out with when I did coke. I've rediscovered me and I've rediscovered my real friends."

Perhaps that all sounds too good to be true. A little corny, maybe. It doesn't matter. Anyone can see that it makes sense and, deep down inside, you know there are notes in Keith's story that relate to your own.

Putting your trust in addiction and drugs is a huge underestimation of your natural resources and human spirit. But as addicts, we give the drug credit for things we otherwise do naturally. The fact is that cocaine is a cowardly, pathetic fool who steals our worth, our strength, our true character and our true selves.

I have a favorite analogy for drug addiction of any sort: nicotine, alcohol, cocaine, cannabis, gambling, anything… I liken it to someone who doesn't have a broken leg buying a crutch that's riddled with termites.

The belief that you need coke as a crutch is keeping you in the trap.

I was once told a story about a remote tribe that, if you drew a white chalk circle around one of them, they couldn't step out of it. They believe strongly that they must stay in the circle, and that belief alone keeps them there. There is absolutely nothing physically holding them in.

You might think they're unsophisticated fools, but you know what it's like to be locked in by a belief. Up until now, you thought it would be hard or even impossible to stop using cocaine, that life without coke would be too horrific to contemplate. Now you need to change your mindset and see that it's fine to step out of the circle. Nothing bad is going to happen. Quite the opposite, in fact. Only good things lie ahead.

HIGHS AND LOWS

As you get sucked deeper and deeper into addiction, the lines get longer and longer and fatter and fatter. Rather than chasing a high, you're running away from a low—a low that cocaine created and a low that each line of cocaine perpetuates rather than relieves. It merely creates the illusion that it relieves it.

You don't choose to use cocaine. If you had any choice in the matter, you wouldn't be reading this book. We all started taking the drug for a variety of foolish reasons—peer pressure, to appear sophisticated or glamorous, or rebellious or outrageous, or simply in the pursuit of hedonism—the desire to feel good.

The fact is that there are plenty of things you can do that are genuinely wonderful, amazing, fun, and enjoyable. There's a danger of doing too much of some of those, but the human brain and body are perfectly capable of regulating our activities.

It's only when chemicals are introduced that we begin to ignore our body's warning signs and push ourselves too far, for too long, too often—to the point of often becoming a 24-hour-a-day occupation. At this point:

THE COCAINE HAS WON.

Everything else—all the fun, all the glamor, all the really exciting REAL fun—drains away, and all we're left with is doing the drug, day in, day out, never being allowed to stop.

For weekly users, it does all of this as it drags us deeper and deeper into the addiction pit until that's where we end up. You've become aware, even if it's just at the back of your mind, that you no longer do it because you like it or because you want to, but because you have no choice. You're compelled to continue against your better judgment.

Rather than chasing a high, you've seen the real situation—that you're running away from a low.

All you need to do is realize that cocaine created that low. The way to get rid of it is to stop using cocaine. The alternative is to keep using, and spend the rest of your life trying to run away from the low, never succeeding, with that low getting closer and closer and your coke consumption getting more and more frequent in an attempt to combat it.

Chapter 5

ADDICTION

Let's pause for a moment to understand exactly how addiction works—exactly how are we fooled into believing that we get some kind of pleasure or benefit from the drug.

One of the reasons why cocaine is so potentially addictive is because it leaves the body so quickly. The total period of cocaine withdrawal is between two and five days, depending on how much you use, how long you've used it, and your body size and makeup. That's even faster than nicotine.

THE TWO MONSTERS

A lot of coke addicts go all week, or even several weeks, without using coke, and between each fix they go through complete withdrawal without even noticing it. The physical withdrawal is actually very mild. Someone who uses coke every day just keeps topping it up. Whichever type you are, withdrawal will be easy.

Think of it as that Little Monster that feeds on cocaine and utters a feeble cry when it doesn't have it. You can destroy the Little Monster simply by starving it to death.

The cries of the Little Monster are so feeble as to be almost imperceptible. It's very easy to ignore them. The problem arises when they arouse the Big Monster.

The Big Monster, which lives in your brain, is the perception that coke gives you some sort of genuine pleasure or crutch. As long as you believe that you can't quit coke without sacrificing something wonderful, the Big Monster will continue to hold you captive.

But killing the Big Monster is easy too. We just need to help you see cocaine for what it really is, rather than the myth, the illusion, that you've been sold.

A STEADY DECLINE

If you go weeks between bouts of using coke, you might have a tendency to consider yourself more of a habitual coke-taker than an addict. It's a combination of that Little Monster (the mild physical addiction) and the Big Monster (the belief that you get something positive from coke, and that it will be hard to stop) that keeps you hooked.

Both monsters are at work whether you use coke every day or twice a month. Deep inside, you know you're an addict—otherwise you wouldn't be reading this book. Follow the instructions and you'll see just how easy it is to be free.

The "habitual" aspect of using coke might put the idea of coke into your mind from time to time after you finish reading this book and have destroyed both monsters. But it won't make you crave cocaine and it won't give you an unpleasant feeling. On the contrary, it will make you smile, because it'll be a reminder that you're free.

The process we go through in becoming addicted has us fooled into thinking that we get a big boost, a high, or a buzz from cocaine.

Unless you were one of those poor coke babies, born with cocaine inside their systems as a result of their mother's addiction, you were complete before you did your first-ever line. You were not born with a cocaine deficiency.

If you were a coke baby, please don't worry—the addiction is easy to break, and the principles of this method still apply to you. The beauty of Easyway is that it makes it easy for everyone to break free, regardless of their history or personal circumstances.

You were complete and normal before you took cocaine. What happens when we take our first-ever line? Does it take us above normal? It might feel like it, but we need to remember the lifetime's brainwashing surrounding cocaine. The excitement, the buzz, the peer pressure, the peer adulation, the rebelliousness of it all.

There's no doubt that that first line makes us feel different, but if you gave it to a child who had never had it before and had yet to be brainwashed into believing the hype, how do you think it would make them feel?

It would be a very unpleasant experience for them.

Let's get to the crux of this with regard to your first line. It wasn't a high as such. Yes, there was a feeling of danger, a feeling of excitement about doing it. And it's a very strong stimulant. Your heart would have been beating too fast, your brain working too fast. There are definitely huge physical responses.

As time passes, the physical withdrawal begins. It creates an empty, insecure, unsettled feeling. You gradually descend to the bottom of the first dip. For the first time you're feeling slightly uncomfortable, slightly unsettled, like something is missing.

You do another line and that slightly empty, insecure, unsettled feeling disappears and you come back up toward "Normal" again. But you don't get quite back to normal—you've let a serious poison, an addictive substance into your body, and it will disrupt and distort the working of your body and brain in a variety of ways.

Can you see how the second line seemed to give you a boost or a high? You did feel better than a moment before, but all you're trying to do is get rid of the unpleasant feeling brought on by the first line.

Now you begin to withdraw from the second line and the empty, insecure, unsettled feeling returns. You find yourself slipping down again, to the bottom of the next dip. A devastating lifetime's chain has started, and there are only two things that can end it: stop taking the drug or stop living.

Pretty soon the empty, insecure, unsatisfied feeling starts feeling normal to us. We spend most of our lives down here. Whenever we take a line, we do feel better than a moment before. But each line takes us further and further away from normality, further and further away from real pleasure, real highs, real life.

The further you descend, the worse it feels. Now you're not just experiencing the physical withdrawal from the drug but on top of that you also have this mental craving. You consider the drug to be a friend, a crutch, a boost, and an essential part of being you.

You feel miserable without it, but in time you also feel miserable and grotesque when you've had it.

The longer you go between fixes, the more precious it seems to become. The greater the illusory boost and the more miserable you feel afterwards—especially if you've developed that "a**hole-on -cocaine attitude" while under the influence, which leaves you feeling ashamed and lonely as soon as you've straightened out.

The trouble is that this misery, because it creeps up on us over the years, seems normal. How on earth do we consider this deterioration of body, mind and spirit as being normal? Rather than blame the drug, we blame the circumstances in our lives, the stress of work or home life, our partner, our age, a whole host of things.

After a few years in the trap, it's really a triple low that feels like our normal: a very slight physical low; the mental craving; and the general misery of being an addict and being left helpless in the trap. Anything better than that low, any slight boost is going to feel like a high, an ally and a crutch. It really isn't any of those things.

It's not so much a high as a temporary and partial relief from the low that we've come to think of as normal. And don't forget that cocaine is a powerful poison, so its overall effect on your mood, your health and your wellbeing, even if you're a relatively intermittent user, is devastating.

Of course it's also a strong stimulant, so initially it might make you feel like it's given you energy, but as with all stimulants, after a relatively short period of using them, they cease to be effective. They make you more tired, more lethargic, and provide only an illusory boost in the process.

The great news is that we get back to "normal" incredibly quickly. You don't have to wait long. Once you've cut off the supply of the drug to the Little Monster, it dies very quickly. The Big Monster dies even faster. It is the Big Monster that keeps you down far below normal. But it's dying as you read this book.

Let's continue to examine the beliefs that cocaine provides a form of pleasure or benefit.

THE ILLUSION OF PLEASURE

It's normally a combination of cocaine and alcohol that leads to these beliefs, and it's time to be honest with yourself. Is the reason you're reading this book a testament to the fact that cocaine has done all kinds of wonderful things for you? Or is the complete opposite true?

Isn't it true that, in fact, it's the failure of cocaine to do any of the things it's reputed to do—block out life, problems, worries, and depression—that has brought you to this point? Start seeing these illusions for what they really are.

WARNING LIGHTS

Since when did blocking out problems and worries solve anything? Eventually, when we sober up, the problems haven't gone away. They're still there and, in all likelihood, they've gotten worse.

Imagine a pilot flying over a mountain range in thick clouds. The pilot knows the plane needs to fly at a certain altitude to avoid the mountains, and gauges the altitude by looking at the altimeter. If the pilot looks at the altimeter and sees that the plane is flying too low, they might feel a momentary surge of panic, but will respond quickly and pull the plane up to a safe altitude.

The altimeter is the constant gauge of danger from the mountains, and as long as it keeps working and the pilot keeps responding, the plane will remain safe.

But suppose the altimeter malfunctions and the little warning light that flashes when the plane drops too low stops working. The pilot thinks everything is fine, but really the plane is hurtling toward the mountains. The pilot is oblivious to the impending danger.

"Blocking out" life, worries and problems doesn't work. It deprives us of our safety equipment and results in more problems and more worries, not fewer. When it's an unanticipated consequence of addiction, it's bad enough. But to deliberately take a drug in an attempt to achieve that condition would be akin to the pilot deliberately tampering with the altimeter to ensure that it doesn't work correctly.

You're not losing the ability to block things out after reading this book, and anyway, that's NOT why you use cocaine. To present it as a reason implies that you have some sort of choice over whether you take the drug. If you had any choice, you wouldn't be reading this book.

The reason you use cocaine is because you're addicted. Any justification you might have for why you use it is simply an excuse, and not one that stands up to scrutiny. As addicts, we try to explain away our inability to quit. We rack our brains attempting to understand why, in spite of the obvious disadvantages, we continue to take the drug, against our better judgment. This lack of a logical explanation reinforces the brainwashing about the drug; we conclude, "The drug must do something for me, otherwise I wouldn't do it."

Addiction steals the brain's ability to distinguish between REAL and fake pleasures, benefits and sensations of relief.

> *"I believed that alcohol and drugs used to help with my manic depression, but it became clear to me that whatever problems I had, in any way, were exacerbated by booze and drugs… and that applies to depression as well as anything else."*

Whatever problems or issues you face in your life, whatever worries or tribulations you have to deal with, once you're free of cocaine you have at least one less thing to worry about. In fact, you'll notice how many of those problems were made worse or even created by cocaine.

FRIEND OR FOE?

Imagine that you met someone at work, or socially, and at some point they announced that they'd had a stroke of luck, and come into some money, and they gave you $100. It would seem pretty weird, but let's say they insist that they want to share their good fortune, and that they really would like you and their other friends to share in their luck. It's $100. It's not going to change your life—but hey, why not go out for a bite to eat or buy something nice for the kids?

Imagine that a month later they did the same thing. It feels a bit more relaxed this time; you figure, you took it last time, so why not? You take the $100 and thank them. Now, imagine that this has happened regularly for months, and then, gradually, the $100 seems to be headed your way every few weeks rather than monthly. Then every couple of weeks. Then every week. Every single week this person gives you $100. You would still find it a little weird, but you would be appreciative and feel indebted to them. You would think of them as an incredibly kind, generous and lovely friend. You would be grateful to them for the help they had given you.

How would you feel if one day, years after they started to give you money, you found out that this "friend" had actually been stealing from you? They would take $200 from your bank account and give $100 of it to you. Every single time they had given you $100, they had just taken $200 out of your account without you knowing.

Would you forgive them?

Would you spend time with them any more?

Would you accept any more supposed gifts from them?

Would you feel grateful?

Dismiss any feelings of gratitude for anything you think cocaine might have done for you. Whatever "pleasure" you thought you were getting was fake, phony; it was deceitful, and it made a fool of you. And it stole from you.

But does it matter whether the pleasure was real or illusory? If it felt like a pleasure or benefit, isn't that enough?

Think about it. While you thought you were getting some pleasure or benefit from cocaine, it was actually robbing you—of your money, your dignity, and your freedom. When you hit that triple low, there is no illusion of pleasure—just a desperate need to relieve the misery of each new low.

LOSING YOUR INHIBITIONS

Shyness is not an unattractive trait. Who would you rather spend time with, someone who doesn't talk much but listens, or someone who talks too much and shows no interest in what you have to say?

Social occasions can make shy people feel vulnerable, but any sense of inadequacy is only in their mind. Brash, talkative, and coked-up people might well hog the limelight and, therefore, create the superficial impression that they're more entertaining than everyone else. In fact, most people are secretly wishing they would shut up and give someone else a chance.

Coke doesn't make us have more fun or make us more interesting; it just removes our ability to tell when we're being dull, rude, arrogant, embarrassing, or obnoxious. In fact, many of the people who come to Easyway looking for help to quit coke will have that as one of their primary reasons for wanting to break free.

COCAINE DOESN'T GIVE YOU ANY POWERS OR ADVANTAGES OR BENEFITS—IT TAKES ALL YOUR POWERS AWAY.

You don't use cocaine because it helps you lose your inhibitions; you use it IN SPITE OF THAT. You don't use cocaine because it helps you have fun; you no longer have fun BECAUSE you use cocaine.

That's why you're reading this book.

"BUT I USED TO GET A REAL HIGH FROM COKE"

Did you? Do you still? Really?

When we first start using coke, it feels like the greatest adventure imaginable. That first time, the rebelliousness of it, the decadence of it, the thrill of the moment. There's no doubt that it's a seminal moment in our lives. Very few people have a laissez-faire attitude toward it when they first use cocaine. We whip ourselves into a frenzy of expectation. In some cases it's an impetuous moment; nevertheless, we fully understand the significance of what we're doing. No wonder we think it feels amazing.

Indeed, something different does happen. There is a change in our brains and bodies. But the expectation of it being amazing is what almost guarantees it will feel that way. Give cocaine to a young person who has no knowledge of the drug, and they would describe a deeply unpleasant and uncomfortable experience.

Of course you've had fun when you've been coked-up, especially if you've managed not to ruin the occasion *because* you were coked-up. But whatever scenarios you recall, those occasions would have been equally fun, equally thrilling, equally amazing without coke.

Do you have doubts about that?

First, remember how much fun kids have without any chemical assistance. Then look at amazing, wonderful, magical situations that have nothing to do with cocaine: love, sex, dancing the night away, exploring the countryside or a city, playing or watching sports, reading, movies, theatre, dining out, catching up with old friends, music… the list is endless.

Then look at any occasion where lots of people are having fun. Whether it's a huge sports event, a huge musical event, a huge wedding or a big party, they all have one thing in common: most, if not all, of the people there, letting their hair down, letting themselves go, letting themselves feel amazing and wonderful and excited, are not using cocaine.

It's time for you to put it behind you, to reconnect to the real you— not the coked-up, used-up, messed-up, hateful version of you. The you that knows how to have a genuinely good time.

"COKE GIVES ME CONFIDENCE"

It's a thin line between confidence (the stuff of champions and winners) and overconfidence (the stuff of losers, braggarts and fools).

We've talked about loss of inhibitions, and making a fool of yourself is one thing (and a very common thing with coke addicts), but there are other situations that lead to more serious consequences.

It's interesting that most people in the grip of cocaine addiction talk about it giving them confidence—that's the drug talking. It's not confidence, it's overconfidence. And can you think of a single significant moment in your life, or anyone else's, where it might be an advantage to be overconfident?

There are none.

Every great coach in sports history puts overconfidence at the top of their "things to avoid" list. It's a terrible, debilitating, destructive state of mind, which has led to the loss of epic sporting battles, literal battles, and careers.

The fact that the drug makes you "feel" interesting is neither here nor there. The fact that in reality you're probably being insensitive, long-winded, rude, impatient, abusive, boorish, aggressive and possibly violent escapes you entirely.

CASUAL SEX

A man from Switzerland attended one of our sessions and said that, as a gay man, he considered an advantage of coke to be that he could have sex with men he wasn't attracted to. Whether you're a man or a woman, straight or otherwise, it's telling that some coke addicts use that kind of thinking to justify their addiction.

At Easyway, we're not judgmental at all. In our one-on-one seminars, it's often the addict's first time talking about what they do and why they feel they do it. It's an interesting area, and often the clients who talk about this kind of "advantage" of using coke express feelings of guilt and deep remorse about having casual sex.

Without going too deeply into the psychology of why they might be inclined to do something that they don't feel good about doing, it's fairly easy to come to terms with that line of thinking. If you fit into that category, it's time to make up your mind. If you feel you want to, or need to, engage in that kind of activity, go for it.

Do it sober. Experience it for real.

Stay safe, think about it, and analyze whether it's really what you want to do and who you want to be. If the honest, sober answer is yes, keep doing it. If not, stop.

Either way, you can do what you want while being entirely free of cocaine addiction.

If you feel guilty about having casual sex, and feel that you need coke to overcome it, then it appears that some kind of puritanical moral standard has been imposed on you by others, by yourself or, most likely, a combination of both.

It's important to identify these as the factors that make you feel the way you do.

Take control. Decide whether the casual sex thing is really "you," and if it is, just do it. The idea is not to use coke in an attempt to assuage your guilt any more—but to simply lose the guilt.

If, as some clients have said, you use coke to help you have casual sex with someone you're not attracted to, well, that's really not a benefit, is it?

A few lines of coke seem to interfere with and disrupt our personal view of morality in those circumstances. It's one of the worst things about the drug, and one reason why you feel so ashamed and wretched the morning after you've made a spectacle of yourself. That's the case whether what you did last night involved sex, or just involved you embarrassing yourself, or being shamefully mean and nasty to others.

The truth is that you no longer use cocaine to make yourself feel good; you want to STOP taking it because it makes you feel so awful.

Chapter 6

EXCUSES

The landscape of coke addiction has changed dramatically in recent years. Back in the 1980s, it was seen as a really dangerous thing to do. Everyone drank alcohol, a lot of people smoked weed and did speed, and a few people dropped acid. But back then, coke and heroin were seen as being almost on the same level as each other. You'd be considered in a different league if you used them.

These days, coke is almost on the same level as marijuana was back then. In most modern cities, it's everywhere—and everyone seems to be doing it. Of course, it's a lot cheaper these days than it used to be. It's roughly the same price now as it was in the 80s, after more than three decades of inflation.

Coke has become lionized and vilified by society all at the same time, a strange kind of contradiction perpetuated by the way it's portrayed on the silver screen and the way that addicts sing its praises.

Remember, using drugs is like someone who doesn't have a broken leg buying a crutch that's riddled with termites. We don't need drugs, because we're not hurt and we're not weak. Despite what we might be led to believe, we are incredibly strong. And drugs don't do what you're told they'll do. In fact, they do the opposite. Seeing through the illusion will set you free.

Cris Hay, a Senior Allen Carr's Easyway Therapist who has been instrumental in developing our programs for alcohol and a host of other drugs, relates a story about someone who was at his college. Let's call him Fred. Cris always thought of Fred as one of the sharpest, most intelligent, brightest people he'd ever met. When he ran into him three years after leaving college, Fred had become completely unhinged.

He didn't make sense, he was incoherent, he had become obsessed with paranoid conspiracy theories and was the shell of the man Cris had known a few short years earlier. Poor Fred.

It doesn't really matter whether we're talking about the way it ravages your mind or your body, whether it's cocaine psychosis or the disintegration of your nose. Coke does nothing for you but harm.

The purpose in telling this story is not to try to scare you off of coke. If such horror stories, or showing photos of nose damage, made it easier for you to quit, then we would show them here, but as it happens, fear doesn't help anyone to quit.

When an addict experiences fear, what do they do? They reach for the drug that caused it.

You don't need to google "uni-nostril" and look at photos of the nose damage cocaine causes, but you do need to stop letting the fear of it keep you trapped.

GETTING HOOKED

These days, Fred is probably vacuuming coke up his uni-nostril. But that's obviously not how it started out for him. We all started out in exactly the same way as Fred: a line here, a line there, only at certain parties. There's normally a honeymoon period with drugs, when we feel like we're getting away with it, that we can take or leave it.

But the natural tendency with all drug addiction is to take more and more. The body develops a tolerance to the drug, so you need to take more of it to have the same effect.

We kid ourselves that we can stop whenever we want, that if our doctor ever warned us that the effect of nose damage is visible and that disaster is imminent, we would be able to quit right away. But sadly, addiction doesn't work like that.

Confronted with fear, an addict is more likely to snort more coke than magically set themselves free. But stepping to freedom is exactly what you're doing by reading this book—and none of it involves fear. It involves wonderful release. After reading this book, you'll look at coke addicts and you won't envy them; you'll pity them, with compassion.

"I CAN TAKE IT OR LEAVE IT"

Well, that's not really an advantage of cocaine use, but we do need to eliminate the belief that we could be someone who can take or leave coke as they please.

Maybe you have a friend who seems to have gone on for years and years, just dabbling here and there, just having a couple of lines every now and then.

There are a number of types of dabbler. First, there are the ones who just lie—they'll tell you they only do the occasional line, but will do four lines while they're telling you. They lie to you and they lie to themselves.

Then there are ones who are rank amateurs. They do it once a year or maybe a few times a year. They don't suffer the illusion of pleasure—they don't really get much out of it, and do it for the show. We were all like that once. They run the risk of becoming a full-on coke addict, but claim they can take it or leave it.

> *KNOWING WHAT BEING ADDICTED TO COKE CAN DO TO YOU,*
> *CAN YOU THINK OF ANYTHING MORE STUPID THAN SOMEONE*
> *WHO CAN TAKE OR LEAVE IT, SIMPLY NOT LEAVING IT?*

You were like that once. Don't envy them.

Then there are coke addicts who fight, day in, day out, using tremendous willpower to limit their intake of cocaine. Either they can't afford to take more or they're so terrified of what it would do to them that they fight it every single day. It's a miserable existence. They hate it when they can't do it, and hate themselves when they can. Don't envy them. It's like being on a permanent diet.

These people have obligations, jobs, demands on their time and energy, or they are extremely health conscious, or whatever. For one reason or another, they are constantly restraining themselves. But such forced restraint can't be sustained forever. Eventually, inevitably, it disintegrates.

Can you see the difference between the different types of dabbler? Some battle to limit their intake because they're terrified of the effect on their work, mind, body and relationships; others would love to use more if those factors were removed. And they're the people who go crazy on coke while on vacation, where those checks on the addiction are removed.

They may all seem different, but they are all the same in that they are all suffering. None of them are getting the coke they crave, and none of them are getting the freedom they really want either. If you recognize yourself in any of the characters we've described so far, please don't worry. Freedom is within your reach, whatever type of coke user you are.

You don't need to worry about any of this stuff any more, but just remember this:

NEVER ENVY COKE USERS.

OVERRIDING OUR NATURAL INSTINCTS

What about cocaine's effect on the way we interact with people? Most normal people, most healthy people, have a checkpoint between brain and mouth, between thought and action, that keeps them out of trouble. But cocaine short-circuits this.

We've established how it appears to reduce inhibitions in the worst possible ways. It's not just the quantity of words that come out of our mouths as we turn into a total motormouth, it's the quality too. People seem to think they're Oscar Wilde, Jerry Seinfeld, Chris Rock, Amy Schumer, Kevin Hart, or Nikki Glaser when they're under the influence of cocaine, when in reality they're being stupid and arrogant, and more often than not quite unpleasant.

Inhibitions are healthy. They keep us safe and allow us to act in the best interests of our own security. At the top of a tall building, it's a feeling of inhibition, of insecurity, that protects us from going too close to the edge and endangering ourselves.

When we interfere with our natural instincts, we cause ourselves tremendous problems. Instead of accepting a feeling of slight insecurity in a secure situation, we use coke and feel overly secure in what has now become an insecure situation.

Let's think about that statement again.

> *INSTEAD OF FEELING A LITTLE INSECURE IN A SECURE SITUATION, WE USE COCAINE, WHICH CAUSES US TO FEEL OVERLY SECURE IN WHAT HAS NOW BECOME AN INSECURE SITUATION.*

Whether it's a situation where you're in mortal danger at the top of a tall building, or you simply feel overconfident and mistakenly show your hand in a business deal, it's not an argument for doing the drug. In fact, it's quite the opposite.

FATAL MISJUDGMENT

This story may upset you. We've included it here not to try to shock you, but to illustrate the danger that lies in using cocaine to override your inhibitions.

A number of years back, on Valentine's Day, I was out with my partner having dinner. The restaurant was full of couples enjoying their meals. There was suddenly an extraordinarily loud bang—we thought there had been an explosion.

What had happened, though, was that someone at a party in the top-floor apartment next door, a couple of floors above the restaurant, was coked up to the eyeballs and wanted to get something from his apartment, which happened to be the top floor apartment on the other side of the restaurant. The restaurant was a one-story flat-roofed building between the two taller apartment buildings.

The man had tried to jump from one balcony to the other and failed. He fell a couple of floors onto the restaurant roof and died. The police told the restaurant workers that, had the guy been sober, he would have known that he couldn't possibly have cleared the distance.

But then, had he not have been under the influence of drugs, even if he thought he could make the jump, he simply wouldn't have tried to. He would have just used the stairs for the sake of his safety.

The worst thing about that story is that the police said that everyone at the party was entirely out of it on one drug or another, and there were people there giggling about what had happened. Someone had died, and people were just giggling about it.

Any drug that does that to you, that both reduces your fear by giving you a false sense of courage and places you in greater danger by messing with all your cognitive faculties, takes you to places that you really shouldn't be going.

Feeling invincible on coke is like a pilot with a broken altimeter. It really doesn't matter how confident you feel, you're putting yourself in mortal danger and are incapable of saving yourself.

"IT'S JUST A HABIT I'VE GOTTEN INTO"

That's an odd claim to make as an advantage of taking a drug.

The words habit and addiction are often used synonymously these days. People talk about a cocaine habit, but there's a clear distinction between a habit and an addiction, and it's absolutely essential that you understand what it is; otherwise you won't fully understand the nature of the trap, and you will remain vulnerable.

With habits, you are in control. They might be unpleasant habits, but you do them because you want to. Habits are easy to break as long as you want to break them.

If we travel to a country where they drive on the other side of the road, we adjust with ease. When we return home, we adjust back again. The important thing is the underlying reason why certain behaviors become habitual.

The reason might be beneficial. If so, why break the habit? It's unlikely that anyone would deliberately get into the habit of doing something that provided them with no benefit whatsoever, unless, of course, they were deluded into believing that the evil was beneficial; as is the case with cocaine addiction.

Cocaine addicts believe that they choose to take it because it gives them some kind of pleasure or benefit; but if at any time they were to take their head out of the sand and list all the advantages and disadvantages of using cocaine, the conclusion would be,

"I'M A FOOL; I HAVE TO STOP DOING IT!"

That's why, deep down inside, all coke addicts instinctively feel stupid.

In fact, they're not stupid. There is a powerful force at play, and it's called addiction.

You've done cocaine a lot, so there might appear to be an element of habit involved. After you've finished this book, the habit might lead the thought to flash into your mind at a party, "Oh, I'll do some coke now," simply because it's something you've done for so long.

When that has happened in the past, when you tried to use willpower to quit, it would have been a horrible moment that opened up the floodgates of desperation and desire and led to a battle, a struggle that you were destined to lose.

But with this method, with the need and desire for the drug eliminated, those moments are easy to brush aside. In fact, they become moments of real pleasure when you remind yourself how lucky you are to be free. So don't worry about the habit.

THE HABIT OF USING COCAINE DIDN'T GET YOU ADDICTED. BEING ADDICTED TO COCAINE GOT YOU INTO THE HABIT OF TAKING IT.

Free yourself from the addiction, and any habitual issues and triggers are easy and enjoyable to deal with.

Chapter 7

WILLPOWER

Just as the willpower method is commonly assumed to be the only way to cure an addiction, those who fail to quit that way, and remain in the trap, are generally branded as weak-willed. In fact, they brand themselves as weak-willed. They assume it is they who have failed, not the method.

Perhaps that's why you feel you've failed to quit before now; because you lack the strength of will. If that's how you feel, then you haven't yet understood the nature of the trap you're in.

Ask yourself if you're weak-willed in other areas of your life. Perhaps you're a smoker, or you eat too much, or you drink too much and consider this to be further evidence that you lack willpower.

There is a connection between all addictions; but the connection is not that they are signs of lack of willpower. On the contrary, they're more likely signs of a strong will. What they all share is that they are traps created by misleading information and untruths. And one of the most misleading untruths of all is that quitting requires willpower.

HOW WEAK-WILLED ARE YOU?

Let's forget that there are probably plenty of examples in your life of how you possess huge amounts of willpower. It's normally strong-willed people who end up addicted to nicotine, alcohol, cocaine and other drugs.

One of the reasons for that is the brainwashing—cocaine propaganda promotes the view that chemical stimulants might help with stress, or energy levels, or pressure, or mental sharpness and so on. You can see how ambitious, hardworking, successful people with huge amounts of willpower might get pulled into the trap in the belief that it might help them.

It takes a strong-willed person to keep doing something that goes against all their instincts, and turn a blind eye to all the potential downsides of the addiction. And think of the extent you go to in order to get cocaine. When you want it, you WANT it, and you would swim across an ocean to get it.

THE HARD WAY

If I saw you trying to open a door by pushing on the hinge side of the door, and I told you that you would find it easier if you pushed on the handle side, but you ignored me and insisted on pushing on the hinge side, I would call that willful, not weak-willed.

With the willpower method, you force yourself into a self-imposed tantrum, like a child being deprived of its toys. When that happens, the child experiences the most violent physical symptoms, in the same way that most addicts do when they attempt to quit using willpower.

It might have surprised you to learn that the physical withdrawal from cocaine—the complaint of the Little Monster—is actually very mild, almost imperceptible, and no more alarming than spotting a bit of fluff out of the corner of your eye on your shoulder. It might distract you momentarily—but you'd have no problem brushing it off... you wouldn't even need to think about it or make a conscious effort to do it.

It's what goes on in your mind that causes the physical discomfort— not cocaine withdrawal.

Let's look at what might have happened in the past when you tried to quit cocaine using willpower. In doing that, hopefully it will explain how easy it will be for you to rewire your brain—essentially rebooting, resetting it, back to pre-addiction mode.

When we talk about "lines of coke," it encompasses any cocaine consumption, whether you snort it, smoke it, rub it on your gums, whatever. The principles of freedom are exactly the same, however you use it, so apply the following to your own cocaine use.

In the past when you tried to quit cocaine, it's been a little like this: You go to a bar or a party or somewhere you would previously have done coke. Suddenly the thought pops into your mind, "I want a line".

Your immediate response is to fight it. You think to yourself, "I can't." Then you feel the physical response: "Aargh!" It's a gut-wrenching feeling. But let's keep it in perspective; it's not torture, either.

The next thing you do is try to push it from your mind. You try NOT to think about it. But the problem with that is simple: if you try NOT to think about something, you think about it even more! If the next instruction was, "Don't think about an elephant," what would be the first thing that came into your mind?

AN ELEPHANT!

So cocaine stays on your mind, and it triggers the thought again, "I want a line," then the next thought, "I can't," followed by that horrible "Aargh!" feeling again. On each cycle the "Aargh!" feeling gets worse and worse as you fight the urge to think about it but think about it even more.

I want a line—I can't—Aargh! No wonder you've found it hard to break free in the past. The willpower method is almost guaranteed to fail.

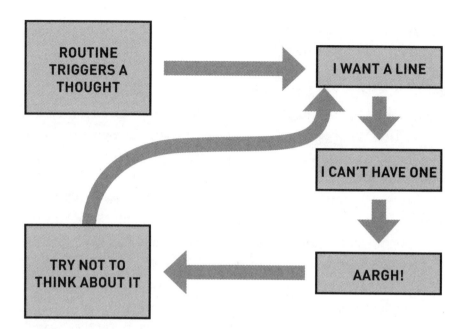

POSITIVE THINKING

By the end of this book, you will understand that there are no benefits, advantages or pleasure in using cocaine. Once you have accepted that, the only natural thought for you to have about cocaine will be, "Great—I'm FREE!"

There will be no feeling of deprivation because you will understand that there is simply no point in using cocaine. It does nothing for you. It only harms you and makes you unsafe. And this time, at the party, or in the bar, or wherever you might have done coke before, if the thought "I want a line" pops into your head out of habit, your reaction won't be "I can't," it'll be:

"GREAT—I'M FREE!"

You won't have to try not to think about it, because the more you think about it, the happier you will be.

GIVE YOURSELF A BREAK

For a little while after quitting, you just need to cut yourself some slack. Understand that it's perfectly normal for a habitual thought to pop into your head. You might think, "I want a line," or you might even forget you're free and think, "I can't," but at that stage, rather than worrying about it, or fighting it, it's a great moment to rebalance yourself and rather than feel "Aargh!" think "GREAT—I'M FREE!"

It might seem a little hard to believe now, but understand this: the "Aargh!" feeling has nothing to do with withdrawal; it's all about what's going on in your head. This rewiring of your brain feels fabulous, and turns moments of potential misery into moments of pure joy.

During the course of this book, you are getting rid of the "want," so there is no genuine "I want a line," only habitual thoughts that are easy to process.

Strong-willed high achievers fall into the addiction trap: business leaders, professional athletes, movie stars, politicians. You don't use cocaine because you're weak-willed, you use cocaine because you're addicted to it. The great news is that, once you know how, the addiction is easy to break.

All you need to do is follow the instructions.

THE TUG-OF-WAR OF FEAR

All addicts have a tug-of-war going on in their minds. Coke addicts are no exception. On one side, we know all the downsides of the addiction: it's killing us, costing us a fortune, enslaving us, causing us to lose our emotions, lose our friends and loved ones, leading us into ever more risky, ever more shameful situations, making us paranoid and doing who knows what else to our brains. On the other side of the tug-of-war, we worry about how we would cope without cocaine: how could we enjoy life, handle social occasions, handle work and stress, and keep living our lives?

It's the fear of what will happen to us if we keep using coke versus the fear of what will happen if we stop. How will we cope? Fear is on both sides of the tug-of-war.

Do you recognize that conflict? I'm sure you do, to a greater or lesser extent. It never occurs to us as addicts that the cause of the fear at both ends of the rope is the drug.

COCAINE DOESN'T RELIEVE THE FEAR; IT CAUSES IT.

If we can banish both of those fears, the drug loses its grip.

The fear of the harm coke is doing to you is going to disappear the moment you are free. So that's great news. And the fear of what's going to happen when you quit will be banished as you continue to read this book.

Nothing bad is going to happen. The scary stories you've heard about how hard it might be to quit, and the bad experiences you've had in the past when you tried to quit on your own, are all based on one thing: willpower.

The people you've seen struggle and fail to get free, perhaps yourself included, were trying to do it the hard way. This way is different. Hopefully you're sensing that already. If not, don't worry—you will.

If you can get the truth into your mind—that you get no pleasure or benefit from cocaine—then you won't feel deprived and miserable when you quit. You'll feel:

FREE!

That might sound a little far-fetched right now, but I have only good news for you. All you need to do is keep reading and follow the instructions.

Chapter 8

RECONNECT WITH YOUR NATURAL FACULTIES

There are a whole host of other benefits you might believe you get from cocaine, besides the most common ones, which we've already dismissed. But let's recap and elaborate a little further.

Rather than ask what cocaine does for you, perhaps the question should be, What does cocaine do TO you?

We've established that it provides you with an initial surge of energy, and that it then deprives you of the ordinary use of your senses and reason. In fact, cocaine affects all our faculties, including self-control.

Most people have a checkpoint between brain and mouth that keeps them out of trouble. Cocaine, even more so when combined with alcohol, short-circuits this. It impedes inhibition, and that is not useful, positive or desirable. It makes us behave in all sorts of ways that we wouldn't dream of if we were not under the influence of the drug.

This is the very worst thing about cocaine. It's what makes people indulge in phony displays of affection or the opposite, anger, to complete strangers. And we often reserve the very worst treatment for the most important people in our lives, our loved ones at home.

You might argue that you're a perfectly civilized person when you're on coke, but deep down you know you're not. Isn't that one of the reasons why you're reading this book?

EMBRACING SHYNESS

People use cocaine as a social lubricant because it makes you *feel* like you're absolutely fascinating, exciting and fun. Usually the opposite is true.

If you feel that cocaine helps you in social situations, maybe you feel the real you is a little restrained or even shy. You can overcome that reservation by making a habit of helping other people overcome theirs. Most people love talking about themselves. So ask them questions— about their job, their interests, their kids. They'll think you're a great conversationalist when you've hardly said a word! And there's no gut-wrenching regret about your behavior the next morning.

If you're so shy that this suggestion fills you with panic, take comfort in this: shyness can be a very attractive quality. People would much rather spend time with someone who is a little shy than listen to the hollow bragging of some sweaty, drunken cokehead, all puffed up with a sense of their own importance.

Are we ever fooled by cokeheads? Do we really regard them as go-getting types, facing up to life's big challenges? Or do we see them as sad individuals, rather like those normally timid little men who hog the road once they're cocooned in the safety of a big car?

When Tracy on your volleyball team, usually a meek individual, verbally abuses the bartender over some insignificant detail, do you turn to a teammate and say, "I never realized Tracy was so assertive"?

When Phil from finance starts dancing half-naked on the table at the office Christmas party, do you think, "What a free spirit! I wish I could be like that"?

Do you really desire that phony sense of "confidence" that coke creates? Isn't it the fact that you don't want it that has led you to read this book? The fact is, you probably know how weird and fake and odd you come across as when you're coked-up. And it scares the life out of you.

The really sad thing is that everyone, with the possible exception of the person under the influence at the time, knows it's fake.

The trouble with using coke in this way is that you're really telling yourself that your inner resources don't exist. If, for example, you resort to that kind of "courage," you're telling yourself that you lack real courage. And after a while you start to believe it and act as if it were true.

WHAT IS COURAGE?

Let's take a look at what it means to be genuinely brave. The dictionary defines courage as:

"Acting despite fear."

Is an ostrich being courageous by sticking its head in the sand at the first sign of danger? No, it's removing fear, which is a very different thing from conquering it.

In certain situations, cocaine can temporarily reduce fear, in which case less genuine courage would be required. Therefore, resorting to cocaine in such a situation would actually prevent you from summoning the full force of your own inner courage.

But courage is like a muscle: the more you use it, the more it grows and the easier it becomes to use. Besides, by burying its head in the sand, the ostrich does much more than just remove its fear; it deprives itself of three other faculties essential for survival:

THE ABILITY TO SEE, TO FIGHT AND TO FLEE.

Coke triggers misplaced aggression and paranoia—an impulse to fight when there is no battle and to hide when there is no threat.

Getting coked-up might reduce fear in certain situations, but that actually increases the danger, because it impairs your comprehension and coordination, decision-making and discretion.

When you see the aftermath of terrible tragedies and disasters, you have to admire the first responders who run toward the danger, rather than away from it. They don't need cocaine to give them courage, and cocaine would render them less effective at their job.

Remember the pilot flying over a mountain range in fog? If you've ever had to drive in fog, you'll know it's an alarming experience, even at the slowest speed, in daylight. Imagine what it must be like to fly a plane through a mountain range in nighttime fog. Now try and imagine what it would be like if the pilot suddenly realized the radar, altimeter, fuel gauge and compass were malfunctioning. How terrifying would that be?

But can you imagine the pilot deliberately tampering with those instruments, so they give false readings? The plane is flying through fog in a range where the pilot knows the peaks reach 4,000 feet. The altimeter registers the plane's altitude at 2,000 feet, so the pilot adjusts its calibration so that it reads 5,000 feet.

That's effectively what we're doing when we consume cocaine to mask our fear.

If you knew the situation required you to employ your mental and/ or physical faculties, the fear would be increased. Why? Because while an ostrich might fool itself by burying its head in the sand, the pilot would know that by interfering with the instrument panel the plane had been placed in even greater danger. So in this case the fear would be magnified. The only way the pilot could remove the fear would be to take action: to increase the altitude. In fairness to ostriches, it's a myth that they bury their heads during times of danger. Any species that adopted such a stupid tactic would be highly unlikely to survive.

FEAR IS GOOD

Like all animals, we are completely dependent on our senses and instincts. We think of fear, inhibition, stress and nerves as debilitating evils, but they are vital components of our instinctive survival mechanism. Use a drug to meddle with them, and you're embarking on a course as suicidal as the pilot who tinkers with his altimeter.

There are people born without normal instincts: without inhibition and fear, without any qualms about harming themselves or others. They act like the worst kind of cocaine fiend, even when they're sober. Most of them are in institutions, for their own good and that of society.

There are also people born without senses: completely blind, deaf, with no sense of taste, touch or smell.

Would you envy such a person?

Would you get in a car with a blind driver at the wheel?

People who live with disabilities are aware of their limitations and adjust accordingly, whereas even small amounts of cocaine impair your faculties infinitely more than you realize at the time.

Cocaine has a similar effect on wit: everyone thinks they're a comedian when they're drunk and coked up, when in fact, at best, they're just repetitive and incoherent; at worst, they're offensive, unkind, acerbic, cutting and mean.

Unfortunately, this effect is not limited to social skills: coke makes you feel more competent in every department, while rendering you far less so. The real evil of cocaine is that it places users in dangerous situations while reducing their awareness of risk. Have you taken someone home at the end of the night, or gone home with them and regretted it with all your heart? Did you do things with people or to people that you wouldn't have dreamed of doing when not under the influence of cocaine? Not in an interesting, liberating kind of way either. Haven't you put yourself and/or the people you've been with in dangerous and risky situations that you've deeply regretted afterwards?

We established earlier that even the most foolish ostrich would not attempt to remove its anxiety by sticking its head in the sand. But let's go with the myth that it might. The pilot would know that tampering with his instruments would place him in greater danger, so in his case the anxiety would be increased.

In certain situations we are like the mythical ostrich; in others we're more like the pilot. In some situations cocaine will reduce anxiety, in others it will increase it—normally when the complete opposite behavior is most appropriate. The paranoia that often accompanies cocaine addiction gets worse and worse, more and more severe, debilitating and damaging.

Paranoia aside, imagine you're in the middle of a coke binge when you receive a call from your boss, from an important client, or from a relative. They have a serious problem and are looking to you for help. At that point you would become the pilot: your anxiety would be increased because you would know that in your incapacitated state you are less capable of solving the problem. You would also have to go through that embarrassing farce of pretending to be straight, when it is blatantly obvious that you're not.

Think of your acquaintances. Who are some of the most stressed and nervous? Aren't they the people who use drugs such as cocaine, alcohol and nicotine to try to cope with stress and nerves? Not only do the drugs not help achieve that, they actually make the situation worse.

But a little bit of stress and nerves can be useful as a stimulus to take action. They're part of the human security system.

We treat nerves as if they were a disease, rather than a healthy faculty of a fully functional human being. If the door slams and we jump, we tend to say, "Oh! My nerves are bad!" But that's a sign of good nerves.

Have you noticed how nervy birds are when feeding? The slightest sound sends them to the safety of the trees. That sound might be a cat. It's not only natural for birds to react like that, it's essential to their survival.

And stress is no more evil than a fire alarm. If you're worried about something, that's an early warning signal, and it makes you do something to ward off the threat. It was your anxiety about your cocaine addiction that made you pick up this book in the first place. And this is the most important point of all.

IF COCAINE WAS MAKING YOU CONFIDENT AND BRAVE, DO YOU THINK YOU'D BE READING THIS BOOK?

Coke and booze may appear to take the edge off inhibitions, fear, nerves, and stress at the time, but it magnifies them many times over the morning after. Cocaine is not always responsible for the actual situation that's causing anxiety (although it often is), but it's coke that makes the situation seem like a big deal, rather than a challenge you can deal with.

"CAN'T I JUST CUT DOWN?"

You've probably tried cutting down on your cocaine consumption before. Did it work? Did it make you a happy cocaine user? Of course not. Why? Because that's not how drug addiction works. You don't become less addicted by taking the drug in any measure. As long as you keep feeding it, the nature of addiction is that it gets worse and worse and worse.

Some coke addicts believe they just got into the "habit" of using coke and in particular of taking too much coke, too often. Because we assume that there are such things as "normal" coke users, and that at one point we perhaps felt we were one, we think that if we can get back into the "habit" of just having a couple lines every now and then on the weekend, we'll be able to keep it at that level.

People cling to that theory for years, as week in, week out, they prove it to be an impossible myth.

The very notion of cutting down begs the question: what are you going to cut down *to*? Two lines per weekend? Why not four or three? What the question really amounts to is: which line is the point of no return, beyond which it's hard not to have another and another and another? Is it the third? If so, why not the fourth or second? And surely it depends on the fatness of the line. Besides, how can you gauge that point when your judgment has been affected by a drug?

But let's assume you could, and you figure out that this particular line, of this particular length and fatness, is the one that does the damage. So your rule tonight is two skinny lines and no more. The trouble is, those two lines would make you *care* a hell of a lot less about the consequences of cocaine. So what's to stop you from saying, "Forget the rules! I'm having another"?

Anyone who has tried to cut down will know it never lasts, because cocaine consumption is not habit but drug addiction. You become increasingly tolerant to the drug and need more and more to achieve the same effect. Even to *maintain* your current level you would have to use willpower for the rest of your life. But let's imagine for a moment that you *were* capable of doing that. Let's imagine you *could* use self-discipline and limit yourself to, say, two lines per weekend. Wouldn't your whole life become dominated by those two lines?

Why would you want to put yourself through the agony of that? Do you really want to spend the rest of your life wishing it away for your next fix?

Put it this way: does dieting make food seem less precious, or a thousand times more so? And how long do you think the average diet lasts? Weeks? Days? Hours? Minutes?

So if it can be that difficult to control your intake of food, which you believe *doesn't* mess with your mind, how could you possibly hope to control the intake of a drug that you know removes self-control, self-awareness, caution and care?

It's futile to attempt to exercise control over your cocaine consumption. More importantly, once you know the truth about the addiction, it's entirely undesirable to attempt to do so.

Everyone who reads this book does so for one of two reasons: either they've proved to themselves that they can't cut down or control their cocaine consumption; or they're on the verge of being able to do so, albeit with the odd blip, but it's such hell they can't take it anymore. In either case, it's probably dawned on them that they'd rather be completely free.

Cutting down is not an option. But that's not a problem, because there are no advantages to consuming *any* amount of coke, so you have absolutely nothing to lose by stopping completely.

"COKE MAKES LIFE MORE FUN"

Does it? Really? There's an easy way to find out. When some charmless, drunken cokehead is threatening or belittling people in a bar or at a party, what is your initial reaction?

Is it, "Quick! Give him some more coke and booze!"?

Would that make him twice the fun? Of course not!

And the trouble with addictive drugs is that they get even less "effective" as you develop tolerance. Just as rats develop a tolerance to rat poison, your mind and body get used to the effects of cocaine. You become increasingly resistant to the effect of the drug, so to feel the same effect you have to take more. The drug becomes less and less effective, so you take more and more. That's the way addiction works.

No doubt you can think of plenty of problems, minor and major, that have been caused by your cocaine problem, but can you think of one single problem of yours that was genuinely solved by it?

You can probably remember many enjoyable evenings when you did coke, but what made them enjoyable? The company, the music, the entertainment, the setting and the weather all play a big part in how enjoyable an occasion might be. But can you think of one single event that sticks in your memory purely because of the sheer quality of the coke and the effect it had on you?

Let's face it, the fabric of society is soaked in booze. In some communities it's sprinkled with coke too. Births, christenings, Easter, Christmas, birthdays, graduation ceremonies, weddings, vacations and funerals. For some, a social event without alcohol and coke sounds like a contradiction in terms.

But with the exception of funerals, these are all extremely enjoyable occasions in their own right. If a group of friends is enjoying themselves at a birthday celebration or in a bar, it's not because they're consuming alcohol and/or coke. It's because they're having fun with people whose company they enjoy.

There's exactly the same atmosphere among players in the locker room after winning a football game, when no alcohol or cocaine has been consumed. They don't need alcohol or coke to be happy. They're on a genuine high from the moment the game ends. Often they don't even drink the Champagne that's passed around; they spray it all over each other instead!

The motto that nearly killed Paul Merson and Tony Adams, two of the leading English soccer players of the 1980s and 1990s was, "Win or lose, on the booze!"

For Paul, that normally included cocaine too. But does the atmosphere in the losers' locker room switch from gloom to delight when they have a drink and a line of coke? Paul and Tony are great examples of two supremely skilled, highly competitive, high-achieving international athletes who were not just compromised by cocaine and booze but were brought to their knees, leaving them bawling their eyes out in public, alone, penniless and lost. There is nothing glamorous or fun about cocaine—it steals everything.

The fact that both men have survived and rebuilt their lives is a testament to their spirit.

"COKE GIVES ME ENERGY"

Some people love going to parties. They could dance all night, and often their partner has to pull them off the dance floor in the early hours of the morning to get them to go home. They have the time of their life. But if they've been using coke, they give credit for that energy and stamina to the drug. The fabulous news is that after you've finished reading this book you'll be free of cocaine. You don't have to stop partying and having fun. You're not giving up living; you're not giving up anything. You're getting rid of a disease called cocaine addiction.

WILL I HAVE TO QUIT ALCOHOL TOO?

We've talked a lot about the link between coke and alcohol, and maybe you're worried that you will have to avoid alcohol after you've quit cocaine. That is not at all necessary. It's a personal decision. You can keep doing exactly what you normally do, minus the cocaine.

If you drink alcohol, you can keep drinking. If you smoke marijuana, you can keep doing so. The really important thing is that you not substitute. In other words, don't drink or smoke more than usual in an attempt to replace cocaine.

The caveat to this is if you feel you have a serious drinking issue that you also want to resolve. If that is the case, and you feel confident and empowered after reading this book, by all means commit to leaving alcohol behind too. If at some point in the future you think alcohol is causing problems, we can help you with that, too.

Imagine what the effects of cocaine would be like to someone who had never heard of it; somebody who had never been brainwashed or warned about those effects, and had never had a chance to build up a tolerance to them. Imagine they were tricked into consuming a large amount, and suddenly found themselves unable to think, move, see, or talk normally!

Do you think they would enjoy the experience?

Of course not.

Chapter 9

THE INCREDIBLE MACHINE

Let's return to the pilot analogy one last time.

Imagine being a passenger on that flight through the fog, and watching the pilot snorting a fat line of coke. Would that reassure you or scare the living daylights out of you?

So why is it OK to do it to yourself?

You're the pilot of your plane. The human body is a highly complex machine. It automatically supplies adrenaline and other substances when we need them, and in the quantities we need. As for your brain, it's a far more sophisticated computer than anything you'll find in the most modern airplane.

Do you really believe you can improve on something that ingenious by consuming a chemical that radically affects its natural functions?

We're given incredibly strong bodies. Unfortunately, we tend to mistreat them terribly. We smoke, take alcohol and other drugs, avoid exercise, overwork, deprive ourselves of sleep, gain weight and starve our body and brain of real nutrition. Some do all these things and more for years, or even decades.

Yet our bodies survive in spite of the abuse we subject them to. What an incredible piece of machinery the human body is! And how incredibly strong it is if we treat it with respect.

The human body is the result of three billion years of trial and error, and is by far the most sophisticated survival machine on the planet. When we're young, we're aware of the physical power and strength of our bodies, but as we grow a little older we become physically and mentally weaker. We know that our lifestyle is probably not helping, and that we could eat more healthily, get more sleep, avoid drinking too much, avoid drugs and avoid putting other toxins into our bodies.

But to some extent we've been brainwashed into accepting some kind of decline into old age, in some cases when we're not even out of our 20s or 30s.

Let's just pause for a moment to consider the incredible strength, power and sophistication of our bodies. Could you do the laundry, make the bed, answer the phone, write an email, do the grocery shopping, cook dinner and wash the car? Of course you could; but could you perform all those tasks at the same time?

Now consider the thousands of tasks that our bodies perform automatically, all at the same time, even as we sleep.

The heart has to keep pumping, never missing a single beat. Blood must carry oxygen, energy and nutrients to every part of the body. Our internal thermostat has to maintain our body temperature at the correct level. Every one of our organs, including the liver, lungs and kidneys, have to continue to function in harmony. The stomach must digest our food. The intestines must distinguish between food and waste, extract the former and eliminate the latter.

Any good doctor will tell you that your greatest ally in fighting infection and disease is not the doctor, or any drugs they can prescribe, but your immune system, which, while the above functions are being carried out, automatically supplies chemicals such as adrenaline and dopamine to different parts of your body at the time and in the quantities that it needs them.

Our knowledge of the human body has expanded vastly in the last 100 years. We can transplant organs and achieve mind-boggling results with genetic engineering. However, the greatest experts on these subjects admit that this increased insight into the functioning of the human body makes them realize how little we understand about the workings of that incredible machine.

EQUIPPED TO SURVIVE

All too often it has been shown that, in the long run, the interventions we undertake with our limited knowledge cause more problems than they solve. If your highly sophisticated computer developed a fault, would you let a gorilla try to fix it?

The human body is by far the most powerful survival machine on the planet. It's a million times more sophisticated than the most powerful spacecraft made by humankind. If we abused our cars as we abused our bodies over the years, they would break down and need to be scrapped in no time.

The human body is the culmination of over three billion years of trial and error, all designed to achieve one object and one object alone:

SURVIVAL.

Three billion years is an awful lot of research, and when so-called intelligent people contradict the laws of nature, without knowing the exact consequences of their actions:

THEY ARE CERTAINLY NOT BEING INTELLIGENT.

Our every instinct and guiding force is to ensure that we survive. It's that instinct that has caused you to question your consumption of cocaine.

We think of tiredness and pain as evils. On the contrary, they're warning signs. Tiredness is your body telling you that you need to rest. Pain is telling you that part of your body is being attacked, and that remedial action is necessary.

We think of hunger and thirst as evils. On the contrary, they're alarms: your body is warning you that unless you eat and drink, you will not survive. Each of our senses is designed to ensure that we survive. We're equipped with eyes to see danger, ears to hear danger, a nose to smell it, touch to feel hot or sharp surfaces, and taste to know the difference between food and poison.

Many doctors have discovered that drugs like Valium, Xanax, other Benzodiazepines and medication cause more problems than they solve. These drugs have a similar effect to alcohol. They might take the person's mind off of their problems, but they don't cure them. When the effect of the drug has worn off, another dose is required. Because the drugs themselves are addictive poisons, they have physical and mental side effects, and the body builds an immunity to the drug so that its blocking effect is reduced.

The addict now has the original stress, anxiety and other issues, plus the additional physical and mental stress caused by feeling dependent on the drug that is supposed to be relieving the stress and anxiety.

Eventually the body builds such an immunity to the drug that it ceases to even give the illusion of relieving stress. All too often the remedy is now either to administer larger and more frequent doses of the drug, or to subject the patient to an even more potent and dangerous drug. The whole process is an ever-accelerating plunge down a bottomless pit.

Some doctors still defend such drugs by maintaining that they prevent the patient from having a nervous breakdown in the short term. Again they focus on removing the symptoms.

A nervous breakdown isn't a disease. On the contrary, it's a partial cure, and another warning sign. It's nature's way of saying, "I can't cope with any more stress, responsibility or problems. I've had it up to here. I need a rest. I need a break."

The problem is that many people often take on too much responsibility. Everything is fine as long as they're in control and can handle it. In fact, they often thrive on it. But everyone has phases in their life when a series of problems coincide. Observe politicians when they're campaigning before an election. They are strong, rational, decisive, and positive. They have simple solutions to all our problems. But when they achieve their ambition, you hardly recognize them as the same person. Now that they have the actual responsibility of being in office, they become negative and hesitant.

No matter how weak or strong we are, we all have bad patches in our lives. The usual tendency at such times is to seek solace through what we've been brainwashed to regard as our traditional crutches: alcohol, nicotine, cocaine and other drugs. It might be normal, but there's absolutely nothing rational about it.

The only answer to stress is to remove the cause. It's pointless to pretend that stress doesn't exist. Whether it is real or illusory, drugs will only make the reality and the illusion worse.

HANDLING STRESS

Another problem is that we are brainwashed into believing that we lead very stressful lives. The truth is that the human species has already successfully removed most of the causes of genuine stress. We no longer have a fear of being attacked by wild animals every time we leave our homes, and the vast majority of us don't have to worry about where our next meal will come from or whether we'll have a roof over our heads.

Imagine being a rabbit. Every time you pop your head out of the burrow, you not only have the problem of finding food for yourself and your family, you also have to avoid becoming the next meal of another creature. Even back in your burrow you can't relax or feel secure, because you're threatened by floods, ferrets and other hazards— including those imposed by mankind.

The stress of serving in the Vietnam War understandably caused many service people to turn to drugs. But they served for a comparatively short period. How does a rabbit survive Vietnam levels of stress its entire life, yet still manage to procreate at a prolific rate and feed its family? The average rabbit even looks considerably happier than the average human being!

The reason why rabbits can deal with all this stress and trauma is because they have adrenaline and other drugs occurring naturally. They also benefit from possessing the powers of sight, smell, hearing, touch, taste and instinct—everything they need to survive. Rabbits are extraordinary survival machines:

BUT THEY'RE NOT AS EXTRAORDINARY AS HUMAN BEINGS.

We have reached a stage of evolution whereby we can even partly control the elements. Properly organized, we could virtually eliminate the effects of droughts, floods and earthquakes. We really have just one substantial enemy to conquer:

OURSELVES.

At our stop-smoking centers we ask smokers, "Do you have a smoker's cough?" Often the reply is, "No way. I would stop smoking if I did."

But a cough isn't a disease; it's another of nature's survival techniques to eject harmful deposits from our lungs. Vomiting is another survival technique, to eject poisons from our stomachs.

Taking a drug means that you are altering the calibration of one or more of your senses—the instruments on which your wellbeing depends. The increased security, courage, confidence and happiness we experience when we free ourselves from addiction is truly priceless.

But we are more than mere machines run by computers. The resourcefulness of the human spirit is phenomenal. Look around you. Every single day, so-called ordinary people act with astonishing heroism, and they're not using cocaine to do it.

A huge number of US military service people returned home from the Vietnam War in the 1970s after using heroin for the duration of their service there. They were seriously addicted to the drug. Hundreds of thousands of them.

Yet studies concluded that more than 90 per cent got free of the addiction overnight. Without any problems at all. With little, if any, support at all. With professional support, that percentage would doubtless have been even higher.

You're about to be set free overnight too. Easily, without any pain and without feeling any sense of loss.

"WILL LIFE BE ENJOYABLE AFTER I QUIT?"

With all addictions, it's not just where you're going that is so important; it's what you are escaping from that counts.

All those coke-fueled nights out? There is something that beats them hands down: partying and dancing all night with friends without the need or desire to consume an addictive, toxic substance that regularly makes you feel moody, anxious, paranoid, sad, terrified, ashamed, and regretful. Freedom from a drug that makes you feel ill, exhausted, and generally lousy, and controls you while costing you and your loved ones an absolute fortune.

The real pleasure in those good-time situations always came from the company of your friends, the party atmosphere and the dancing. You can keep doing all that with beautiful abandon.

From now on, it's all guilt-free. It's all fun.

Cocaine has been "hitching a ride" on the back of these wonderful components that make up the moment. Now you can be a party animal without the need for drugs.

That said, you'll probably be amazed at how many dull, drab, boring events and people you can happily choose to avoid after you quit. All those places and people you sought out simply to feed your addiction? You won't need them any more. You'll get your choice back.

"DOESN'T ADDICTION STAY WITH YOU FOR LIFE?"

Dismiss the scaremongering that other so-called "experts" spread about addiction. They might mean well, but they are unwittingly adding to the fear and confusion surrounding the subject.

Addiction is not an all-powerful, mystical phenomenon or a permanent illness or condition that you can never free yourself from. At its root is a simple misunderstanding. Your brain mistakes the drug as the thing that provides relief from cocaine withdrawal when in fact it's the cause of it.

This backward thinking allows the brainwashing to take root and grow in your mind. That is the illusion that coke provides you with a genuine pleasure or crutch. This leads to a feeling of deprivation when you try to cut down or quit.

I once said to someone I was helping get free of cocaine, "Why don't you just think of yourself as someone who, by definition, under no circumstances ever takes drugs, and move on with your life?"

Imagine being in a place where you could do that. Well, you're nearly there. And far from feeling a sense of sacrifice or regret or loss, when you are finally free of coke, you'll barely be able to resist shouting from the rooftops about how happy you are.

Whether you've been doing coke for a few years or for decades, this program will set you free. If you haven't lost everyone and everything already, good for you. You're about to get out just in time. If, on the other hand, you're on your own, alone, and have already lost it all, don't worry.

"THE GIFT OF FREEDOM WILL BREATHE FRESH LIFE INTO THE DISASTER AREA YOU CALL YOUR LIFE"

By the way, those are the words of one of our recent clients, not our own. Whatever your history with cocaine, the future is all of a sudden looking extremely bright for you.

Chapter 10

GETTING FREE

How many times have you blown your rent money, your partner's money, your mortgage money, or simply borrowed money from anyone gullible enough to lend it to you, just to buy coke?

You've felt ashamed and useless and at rock bottom. You've said, "Never again. I simply can't do this any more." And you might have cried and felt ashamed and curled up in your bed. But what happened a week later? Or a few weeks later? You were back on it.

Start seeing your addiction like that tribe's white chalk circle I mentioned earlier. You can step outside it forever, any time you want to. Human beings are good at seeing other people's white chalk circles for what they are, but we need our own chalk circles to be pointed out to us. It's now time to start seeing your own for what it is.

As coke addicts, we completely overestimate the things we think the drug does for us. We're fooled into believing it gives us courage or energy or confidence when, in fact, it does none of those things. In your heart, at this moment, you know it does the complete opposite.

All you need to do is see the drug for what it really is. Acknowledge how you became brainwashed and conned into believing it gave you some kind of pleasure or benefit.

You understand that withdrawal pangs are very mild and barely noticeable. There is no danger whatsoever. Cocaine withdraws from the body incredibly quickly—in three to five days. There's nothing to it. Withdrawal is easy.

It's what happens in your mind that creates unpleasantness, and that only happens if you follow the wrong method.

ANYONE CAN QUIT

You're not addicted because you're stupid or weak. Highly intelligent people seek our help for this addiction, and many of them have excelled in their chosen field or profession. You don't attain that kind of business, musical, sports, media, legal, medical, or creative success if you're stupid, weak or lacking in willpower.

Amazingly, just like you, the addiction convinced them that coke played a part in their success. They seek our help because it's actually playing a part in dismantling it.

It was the addicts' natural talent, hard work, spirit and drive that got them to the top, and coke seemed to be one of the trappings of their success. They realize too late that, rather than giving them energy, it destroys it; rather than giving their personality a lift, it makes them arrogant and boring; and rather than being in control of their coke use, the drug is in control of them.

John Steinbeck's classic novel *Of Mice and Men* perfectly describes our relationship with drug addiction. Lenny worships George partly because he saved him from drowning in a river. Poor Lenny is so slow and mentally challenged that he entirely disregards the fact that it was George who pushed him to go into the river in the first place, in the full knowledge that he couldn't swim and would certainly drown if not rescued. Lenny remains blindly grateful to George in spite of the facts.

No matter how low cocaine drags us down, as addicts we remain grateful for the perceived pleasures we're conned into believing it provides. It ends up as a triple low: first the very slight physical withdrawal; then the mental craving that is triggered by it, making you feel constantly irritated, deprived and miserable; and on top of that the drug drags your body, mind and spirit to greater and greater depths, destroying relationships, careers and friendships.

And all of that—all of it—ends up feeling like NORMAL. A constant state of misery and dissatisfaction.

When you had a line, it seemed to make you feel better for a moment. That's how drug addiction works. Looking back, you can probably remember yourself doing a line to perk yourself up, then at some point feeling you needed to settle down a little, so you had more booze, then another line, and booze, and maybe smoking weed too. A roller coaster of ups and downs.

It's anything but glamorous and, as you already know, people who are coked up might feel like the smartest, most accomplished, most exciting and interesting person in the room. But the fact is that they're normally acting like the dullest and most boorish oaf in the world.

Our experiences when we try to quit with the wrong method do tremendous harm to us. If we go to Narcotics Anonymous, the first thing we're told is that the we are powerless over our addiction. Great! We're basically told to surrender to the addiction and acknowledge that we have two options: fight a lifelong battle or submit to the drug and die.

That's exactly like telling someone who thinks they're trapped by a white line of chalk around them that they are trapped in that circle. But that person doesn't need to take 12 steps, she just needs to take one— the simple step of crossing the white chalk line.

FORGET CUTTING DOWN

Remember what we've learned about dabblers. We meet a variety of people who seem to get away with only having a line of coke every now and then, and it's important that you don't envy them.

There are a few different types. First, the liars. They'll tell you they only do a line or two a month and never feel inclined to have more. But you notice they've already done a couple of lines, and they go on to do a few more while you're standing there watching them.

They lie to themselves and everybody else.

Then there are the very occasional users. They barely ever have a line. If nothing else, they prove how weak the addiction is. They've gone through complete withdrawal every time they've occasionally done it. Often, if they're honest, they don't even enjoy the experience of doing it. They don't like being wired, so it puts them off for another six months.

They're playing with fire. And if you're honest, isn't that exactly how you started out? They're the fly at the top of the pitcher plant, and it doesn't take much to change in their life for them to fall all the way in. One rough patch and that illusion of self-control disappears.

Then there are the apparently moderate users. Often, like the liars, they normally have more of it, more often than they're prepared to admit. Some of them simply can't deal with more of the poison. Their bodies aren't strong enough to handle the effects. Some can't work if they use coke. Others are afraid of getting caught and losing their job. Drug testing is becoming increasingly common in many industries.

For whatever reason, they are forced to limit their intake of the drug. It's like being on a permanent diet. They wait days and days until they allow themselves to finally have a line—and then another and another. The longer they wait between uses, the more precious it seems to be when they finally cave in.

That's why cutting down doesn't work. That plus the fact that addiction simply doesn't ever get less severe. The addict is destined to take more and more. As your body builds resistance to the poisonous drug, you need more of the drug to have an equal effect.

IT'S NOT YOUR PERSONALITY

Whether you think you have an addictive personality or not, whether you think you have addiction in your genes or not, we have only good news for you. You will still find it easy to stop and stay stopped.

YOU GOT HOOKED ON COKE BECAUSE YOU USED COKE, NOT BECAUSE OF YOUR PERSONALITY OR GENES.

Coke is one of the most addictive substances we know, and guess what: people without addictive personalities or genes, if such things exist, get addicted to it too. The way out is the same for everyone and it's easy for everyone, regardless of your genes or personality.

The theory of addictive personality or genes stems from looking at the situation from the wrong perspective. It's not your personality or genes that get you addicted, it's your belief that you get some kind of pleasure, benefit or crutch from the drug.

Whether you remain convinced that you have an addictive personality or not doesn't matter—this method will set you free, and you'll find it easy to stay free. After all, there are a multitude of former addicts who claim they have addictive personalities and genes but remain free; however, they were not smart enough, or lucky enough, to use the method that makes it easy.

LIFE EXPERIENCES CAN'T STOP YOU FROM QUITTING

Other people say that the reason they got hooked is because they have or had deep-rooted issues in their life. We understand how hard life can be, but with all respect, this is another red herring. There is no doubt that many people are born into incredibly difficult and challenging lives, whether it's a bad childhood, an appalling childhood, a difficult adolescence, or any number of things. Because of the brainwashing that tells us that drugs are a kind of "cure-all" that can lift you out of your environment, people who have had bad experiences on a long-term basis might be more likely to take drugs—but that doesn't make it harder for them to get free.

The simple belief that they're particularly badly addicted or prone to be addicted because of their circumstances easily turns into one of those white chalk circles. It's based on the exact same nonsense. It's as easy for them as it is for anyone to step out of the circle and set themselves free—as long as they use the right method.

Let's examine this argument a little more.

Are there people with deep-rooted issues who use coke?

Yes.

Are there people with deep-rooted issues who have never once used coke?

Yes.

Are there people without deep-rooted issues whose only real problem in life is that they're addicted to coke?

Yes.

Are there people without deep-rooted issues who don't have a coke problem?

Yes.

Can you see how there is no connection whatsoever? Someone who has deep-rooted issues may well also have a coke problem, but the deep-rooted issues are not the cause of the coke problem. If they were, everyone with a deep-rooted problem would use coke, and no one without deep-rooted issues would touch it.

NO MIRACLE CURE

Imagine that you have a pimple on your face. Someone gives you an ointment that they say will clear it up. You rub it onto the pimple and the spot magically disappears.

A week later the pimple returns, only this time it's bigger and redder. You apply more of the ointment and it disappears again. Five days later it returns, but now it's more than just a pimple; it's a rash. As time goes on, the gap between the rash breaking out becomes shorter, and it gets bigger and bigger and itchier and itchier each time.

Imagine the horror you would feel as you realized that it's just going to get worse and worse unless you find a cure. Imagine that you've become so reliant on the ointment that you're prepared to pay a fortune for it, and you have to take it everywhere with you because you're afraid to go anywhere without it.

Then you discover that you are not alone; there are millions of other people suffering from the exact same problem, and they're all handing over a fortune to the ointment industry.

The nightmare goes on and on. Then one day you meet a man who says he used to have the exact same problem but solved it. You ask him his secret and he tells you.

STOP USING THE OINTMENT.

He advises you to do the same thing, and reassures you that the rash and pimples will clear up in a matter of days, and after that

YOU WILL NEVER SUFFER FROM IT AGAIN.

What would you do? Would you feel miserable that you could never use the ointment again? Or would you be elated that you'll never have to?

Now apply this logic to cocaine. You have the power to free yourself. Isn't that a wonderful feeling?

COPING WITH CHANGE

You're going to make an informed decision to get rid of coke from your life. Over time you'll notice some tremendous changes. Your bank account will take a while to look healthier, but *wow*, will it look healthier!

You'll look and feel like a million bucks. Over time you'll realize how much life, energy and vitality coke stole from you. At those moments, remind yourself that you're enjoying normality. There is nothing special about feeling good. It's the least you deserve. It's what you've escaped from that's really important. Always look back and smile about what you've left behind.

Your sixth instruction is simple:

MAKE A WRITTEN RECORD OF HOW COCAINE AFFECTED YOUR LIFE.

Write down what life was like for you as a cocaine addict. What was it about that life that made you want to quit?

Make sure you write it in the past tense. Remember, it is what you have escaped from that's important, not where you're going.

Be expansive. For example, you could say, "Life as a coke addict made me feel unhealthy," which is true, but it is probably more accurate and truthful to say, "Life as a coke addict messed with my body, my mind and my spirit. I felt constantly tired, on edge, and horribly unhealthy. That made me feel miserable and wretched." It is important that you include details of the factors and how they made you feel—all in the past tense, because it is what you have escaped from.

The factors mentioned above are just examples. Make it personal for yourself, in your own words, describing your own feelings.

Do this with all the aspects of your life as a coke addict. For example, you could say, "It controlled my life, what I did, when I did it, and how I felt when I was doing it—and that made me feel weak."

Go to town on this task. Tell it exactly how it was.

Once you've done that for every aspect of your life as a coke addict, keep that record nearby, in your bag, because you'll need to refer to it at certain times.

Be comfortable with the knowledge that you are going to think about cocaine from time to time, even though you probably feel worried that you might think about it too much right now. It's worrying about it that is the problem.

Remember the "I want a line" diagram? If not, go back and read Chapter 7.

If you try not to think about cocaine, you will think about it even more. Remember the elephant!

It's not a problem if you think about cocaine from time to time, even if you think, "I WANT A LINE." That's just a hangover from the habits you associated with your cocaine use. It's very easy to remind yourself that you're free of all that, and rejoice in the knowledge that you no longer need coke.

Some people find this difficult to accept, but it is true. Think about it. If you were arguing with a friend or lover, at the height of the argument you might think, "I COULD KILL YOU RIGHT NOW"— but it doesn't mean you could, does it? It doesn't make you a killer.

It's just a thought, and it's what you do with the thought that matters. Imagine that you parked your car in the same parking space every day for a year. Then one day your parking space was moved one space down. It wouldn't be a big surprise if you parked in the old parking space by mistake, would it? But how would you react? Would you turn the engine off, throw your hands in the air and think to yourself, "DAMN! I'M INFATUATED WITH THIS PARKING SPACE—I'M EMOTIONALLY ATTACHED TO IT—I CAN'T POSSIBLY PARK MY CAR IN THE NEW SPACE!"? Or would you just smile a wry smile and move your car?

Automatically following old habits isn't a sign that you want that old routine back. It just means that your brain has forgotten the new routine momentarily. So if, after you've quit, the thought of using coke comes into your mind, it doesn't mean the Little Monster is winning or that you need to fight anything, it's just a sign that your brain has forgotten that you're no longer hooked. And every time you remember, it's a wonderful moment.

Rather than worrying about it, or panicking about it, or trying not to think about it, welcome the thought and say to yourself, "GREAT— I'M FREE!" and feel good about it. If you need a nudge in the right direction this is an excellent time to read your record of what life was like as an addict.

Put the book down now and write that record. It only needs to a page long. Then carry it with you. It's a wonderful written testimony of what you're escaping from.

We need these reminders because it's amazing how quickly the body and brain forget pain. It's actually part of our survival mechanism. If you could recollect pain and misery exactly how they were at the time, you'd be doubled up in pain every time you remembered the time you broke your leg, or the time you banged your head on a low beam.

For this reason, the brain filters out and dilutes the memory of pain or painful incidents. Be aware of this because once you've quit, something might happen that reminds you about coke or triggers a rose-tinted memory of how life used to be on coke—a phony memory that obscures how bad you really felt. This is where the written record proves invaluable.

Chapter 11

REGAINING CONTROL

People who consider themselves in control of their cocaine use suffer from the illusion of pleasure more than those who realize they've lost control. But ask them to define the pleasure and they can't. Instead, they offer defensive excuses:

"I can take it or leave it."

"I don't do it that much."

"It's not doing me any harm."

If they genuinely enjoyed it, why would they choose to leave it? The only possible reason is that it's causing problems.

If they didn't think their cocaine use was a problem, and it gave them a genuine pleasure or crutch, why not do it more often? Imagine if a friend told you that they only have bananas once a month. Would you think, "There's someone who's in control of their bananas."? Or would you think, "Golly! I didn't know she had a banana problem!"

As for the excuse "It's not doing me any harm," even if that were true, is it any reason for doing something? Wearing a top hat and singing *Yankee Doodle* doesn't do any harm—but would you choose to do it for that reason? It would be crazy. But not half as crazy as giving the excuse that you do coke because it doesn't do you any harm, when everybody knows it does!

LINGERING CONCERNS

As you enter the final stages before becoming a non-cocaine addict, you might still have some lingering concerns. It's time to remove any traces of uncertainty.

If you were taken up in a plane and told to parachute out, you'd feel a lot better about it if you'd been through the correct training, and knew and understood everything you had to do. If you've followed everything in this book so far, that's how you should be feeling now about quitting cocaine.

You're about to experience an exhilarating sense of freedom. That's what you were hoping for when you boarded the plane, and that's what you've been prepared for. You should feel confident about your every move. But it's completely understandable that, as you stand by the door of the plane, looking out at this wonderful new experience that awaits you, you feel butterflies in your stomach and a little knot of apprehension.

For the parachutist, these fears are irrational. Millions of people have done it before, the whole process has been tested, you've been given all the instruction you need, and you know it works. All you have to do is jump. But the butterflies are completely natural.

The same is true of any lingering concerns you might have about breaking free of the cocaine trap. Even though there is no foundation for these concerns, it would be foolish to suggest that they don't exist. It's human nature to feel apprehensive about experiencing something new, even when that experience could be the best thing that's ever happened to you.

Coke addicts wish they didn't use cocaine, but they're also afraid that they will have to go through some terrible ordeal in order to quit, or that life will never be enjoyable again without the drug. Even though they know that coke is making them miserable, these fears cause them to put off what they see as the evil day.

"I will stop, just not right now."

It's no surprise that we have these fears. All our lives, we are led to believe that cocaine provides tremendous pleasure and support, and that addictions are incurable. These myths are ingrained among our beliefs before we even do our first line. No wonder we find it difficult to believe that stopping can be easy.

"WHEN WILL I KNOW I'M FREE?"

Having come this far in the program, you deserve a pat on the back for following the instructions and making a positive move to end your cocaine problem. You'll be eager to get to the end and experience the exhilarating sense of freedom you've been promised, but how will you know when you've achieved your goal?

When will you be able to tell that you've definitely become a non-coke addict?

- When you can go a whole day without coke?
- When you can go a week?
- When you can enjoy social events without cocaine?

All these suggestions assume that you will start off with a feeling of sacrifice or deprivation. If you do, there's no telling how long that feeling will last. The truth is much more straightforward:

YOU KNOW YOU'VE QUIT WHEN YOU NO LONGER FEEL ANY NEED OR DESIRE TO USE COKE.

It's not the one you *think* will be your last, or the one you *hope* will be your last. When you quit with Easyway, there is no doubt, and there is no need to wait. If you follow all the instructions, you will be there by the time you finish this book.

The only way you might regard your final line with uncertainty is if you fail to follow all the instructions or you use the willpower method. Get it clearly into your mind: you won't miss cocaine, and you will enjoy life more and be better equipped to cope with stress when you're free.

People who quit with the willpower method are always waiting for some sign that they're free. They also spend their time suspecting that there could be bad news lurking just around the corner, like a dark shadow stalking their every move.

Imagine going for medical tests because you suspect you might have a terminal disease and being told that you will have to wait months or years for the result. It would be torture—hoping for good news, fearing bad news and spending every day worrying because you simply don't know for sure which it will be.

Now imagine you had to wait the rest of your life for those results. That's what it's like for people who are not sure they've kicked cocaine completely. They are waiting for something that they hope will never happen.

This is why the willpower method makes people so miserable. They have to endure the rest of their lives waiting for nothing to happen. It's hardly surprising that the vast majority fail.

ACHIEVING CERTAINTY

Different people reach this stage of the book in different frames of mind. Some think they understand everything and are sure they're ready to quit. If that's you, great—but let's not jump the gun. If you're still uncertain, don't worry; all will become clear. Whatever your current frame of mind, take the time and care to pay attention all the way to the end of the program.

It's perfectly understandable that so many coke addicts believe that stopping will be incredibly hard. There is nothing stupid or unusual in that belief. We're subjected to this brainwashing all our lives, and then we reinforce it by trying to quit by using the willpower method. All your failed attempts to quit or cut down simply serve to reinforce the belief that stopping requires a superhuman effort.

That desperate craving you get when you're fighting the desire to use coke might conflict with everything you know about the evils of cocaine. But the craving is still very real, and so is the irritability and misery you feel when you use willpower to try to stop.

As addicts, we find ourselves in a state of confusion. When we're forced to consider cocaine use logically, we can easily see that it's a con game, but we still feel a desire to do it, and this creates an inner tension. The fact that we can't put our finger on what exact pleasure coke gives us only serves to increase the confusion.

Remember:

- The desire to use coke comes from the Big Monster—the illusion that the drug gives us pleasure or support.
- The edgy feeling we get when we're without coke is just the Little Monster wanting to be fed.
- The Little Monster was created by using coke in the first place.
- Therefore, using cocaine does not relieve the anxiety, it causes it.

Once you have this clearly in your mind, it's easy to see that if you remove the cause of the anxiety, you will immediately start to enjoy life free of cocaine.

The willpower method is all about fighting through the anxiety, not removing it. In the first few days after quitting, when your willpower is at its strongest, you might have the upper hand in the battle. But over time your resolve is likely to weaken, uncertainty sets in, and the craving increases.

Now your mind is torn in two: one half determined to be a non-coke addict, the other urging you to use coke. Is it surprising that we get so confused, irritable and miserable on the willpower method?

It would be a miracle if we didn't!

Even if you starve the Little Monster to death, without destroying the Big Monster you will remain forever vulnerable to the temptation to use cocaine.

With Easyway, you kill the Big Monster first. You unravel the brainwashing and see cocaine for what it really is: an addictive poison that controls and debilitates those who take it. Then the Little Monster is easy to deal with. In fact, you can enjoy the process, confident in the knowledge that you're destroying a mortal enemy.

REMOVING TEMPTATION

Unless you destroy the Big Monster—the desire to do coke—you remain forever vulnerable to temptation. That's why Narcotics Anonymous is right when it tells its clients they're never cured of addiction. With their method it's true. As long as the temptation remains, there will always be the danger of slipping back into the trap.

AA and NA do amazing work all over the world, and the last thing we'd want to do is knock them, particularly as they've helped so many people. But in this way, Easyway, is different.

A question we're often asked is, "Once I'm cured, will I be able to have the odd line?"

The answer is simple: "Why would you want to?"

If you approach your final line still thinking you'd like to have the odd bump now and then, you haven't followed all the instructions, and the Big Monster still lurks in your mind.

There will be times when you're tested. Other coke users who don't understand the addiction trap will see how confident and in control you are as a non-addict, and will assume that one line won't set you back. What these coke addicts don't understand is that you have absolutely no desire to have a line. But you understand it.

With NA or the willpower method, you're told that one line is all it will take to trip you up and throw you back into the pit. This is correct. The point is that, with Easyway, you have no more desire to have a line than you do to take arsenic.

ENJOYING LIFE

All coke addicts fear that if they take coke out of their life they will take out the enjoyment too. It's easy to see why such a belief would stop anyone from trying to quit. Nobody wants to lead a life of sackcloth and ashes, devoid of pleasure or excitement.

The truth is, coke actually reduces your ability to derive enjoyment or excitement from anything. It debilitates your senses, plays havoc with your judgment, makes you crushingly dull, vulnerable, and insecure, and often results in you being sick, and feeling guilty and ashamed and full of regret.

The brainwashing causes cocaine addicts to have a romanticized image of the drug. Where there have been enjoyable situations involving cocaine, a quick analysis of all the details of that situation will reveal that there were other aspects that made it enjoyable: good company, good food, an attractive setting, entertainment, a happy occasion.

If you can think of occasions like this that you believe have been enjoyable because you were on coke, consider them carefully and try to understand why the drug appeared to enhance the situation. It doesn't take much to see that, in reality, it does the opposite.

Instead of perpetuating the illusion that such occasions won't be enjoyable again without cocaine, remind yourself that you will now be able to enjoy those situations more because you'll be free of three tyrants: the debilitating effects of addiction; the restlessness, anxiety, and guilt that surround craving cocaine; and the misery of knowing that you're an addict.

Most of the time, we're not even aware of how cocaine makes us feel. The only time we're really aware of it is when we want to do coke but can't, or we're doing coke but wishing we didn't have to.

YOUR LITTLE CRUTCH

Just as coke addicts believe they get pleasure from coke, they also believe it provides some sort of support. This is because they tend to turn to coke in times of stress, and regard it as a relief.

There are many stressful situations from which you might see using coke as an escape: a family quarrel, pressure at work, financial problems, or just feeling like you need to let your hair down. You can take yourself away, get high, and put your problems out of your mind.

But sooner or later you have to return to the real world and, surprise, surprise, the problems are still there. In fact, they've usually gotten worse.

If you believe that cocaine provides a support in these situations, what happens the next time such a situation arises after you've quit? Your brain will tell you, "At times like this, I would have had a night on coke." And you will feel deprived that you can no longer do so.

Think about it: have you ever found yourself in the midst of a domestic argument and thought, "It doesn't matter that we're yelling horrible things at each another and it's really painful, because I can just go get coked up and it will be all right"?

Or did the fact that you do coke make the argument worse?

Non-addicts also have to deal with stress, but they're not moping because they can't have cocaine. All you have to do is accept that, like all non-addicts, you will have ups and downs in your life after you've quit, and understand that if you start wishing you could do coke in such situations, you will be moping for an illusion and creating a void.

Anticipate the difficult times in life after you've quit, and prepare yourself mentally so you don't get taken by surprise. Remind yourself that any stress you feel is not because you can't have cocaine. Tell yourself, "OK, today is not so great, but at least I don't have the added problem of being a slave to coke. I'm stronger now."

You will find that the stressful situations in your life will actually feel less severe once you're free.

Chapter 12

REMOVING FEAR

As you prepare for your imminent release from the cocaine trap, it's time to cement a positive, excited mindset.

There is an all-too-common phenomenon of reoffending among convicts soon after they are released from prison. It isn't because they believe they can get away with it this time; it's because they are frightened by the unfamiliarity of life on the outside, and crave the "security" of jail. It's what they know.

If you happened to know an ex-con like that, who was struggling to believe that he could deal with life outside prison, wouldn't you want to take him under your wing and show him how much better life is when you're free?

You'd probably begin by listing all the wonderful things you can do, whenever you want to do them, not when you're permitted to do them. Things like:

- Seeing friends
- Going for a walk in the park
- Going on a trip
- Having a nice meal in a restaurant
- Going to the movies or to see a play
- Lounging around with your partner

Of course, he would know all these things, but he might have forgotten just how enjoyable they are. When you're in prison, and denied the usual pleasures in life, your idea of pleasure changes.

The cocaine trap is a prison. When you're addicted to coke, you lose the ability to enjoy the things you enjoyed before you started using it. The coke-induced illusion of pleasure takes the place of genuine pleasures and becomes the be all end all. But that's all it is: an illusion.

The genuine pleasures still exist, and they're still enjoyable. If you knew an ex-con who was struggling to see this, and risking his freedom as a result, wouldn't you do everything in your power to make him see things as they really are?

If you could do that for someone else, why not do it for yourself? Think about all the pleasures you've enjoyed in your life without cocaine, and start looking forward to fully enjoying those pleasures again.

It will help if you write them down. Your list might look similar to the example above for the ex-con, and the more you think about it, the more you will add to it. Take your time. There's no rush. What's important is that you establish the right frame of mind to quit with a feeling of excitement and certainty.

LOOK HOW FAR YOU'VE COME!

In Chapter 1, we explained how Easyway works like the combination to open a safe. In order to use the combination successfully, you need to know all the numbers and apply them in the correct order.

You might have found that frustrating at the time. You were eager to discover the cure to your cocaine problem, and the prospect of reading this whole book might have seemed laborious. But you have followed the instructions, and now stand on the brink of becoming a happy non-addict. You have come a long way toward achieving the state of mind necessary for you to quit and remain free for the rest of your life.

Congratulate yourself on your achievements. Remind yourself that there is no need to feel miserable; on the contrary, you have every reason to feel excited. You're setting yourself free of a prison that has brought you nothing but misery and stress, and you're choosing a life that will bring you a happiness you may have forgotten even existed.

Perhaps you think that's an exaggeration, and that you have no reason to congratulate yourself. You might still be feeling the effects of your cocaine addiction, and struggling to convince yourself that this is going to be as easy as we claim. It's time to address the fear of success.

THE FEAR OF SUCCESS

The fear of life outside jail can keep the prisoner in the trap. He feels secure in his prison because it's an environment he knows. Even though it's a life of confinement and austerity, he fears it less than the world outside, which is alien and riddled with uncertainty.

When we relate this fear to quitting coke, we have established that the fear is caused by illusions. These illusions have been put in your brain by many influences, each of which has a vested interest in you continuing to be addicted to cocaine. You've been brainwashed into believing that cocaine gives you some sort of pleasure or support.

You're also afraid that the process of stopping will be an ordeal that you will not be able to stand long enough to succeed. Remember, with Easyway you succeed in becoming a non-cocaine addict the moment you finish your final line and feel no desire ever to take the drug again.

Some people see the cocaine trap as a hole in the ground—something you fall into easily but struggle to get out of. But that's not the case. Although it might feel like a deep, dark hole, there's no physical effort required to escape. You simply need to make a choice. It's a simple choice between taking a step backward or a step forward. You can either choose to remain in the trap for the rest of your life, becoming more and more enslaved and miserable, or you can choose the opposite.

There is no benefit whatsoever to being in the cocaine trap. You were lured into it by a set of illusions that were conjured up for you by people with a vested interest in you being addicted to cocaine. You took a step backward. And you've found that it makes you miserable.

SO NOW YOU JUST HAVE TO CHOOSE TO DO THE OPPOSITE. TAKE A STEP FORWARD.

It's as simple as that. The fear of success can only stop you if you continue to believe that you get some pleasure or support from cocaine.

Some of our fears are instinctive. For example, the fear of heights, fire, or the ocean are natural responses that protect us from falling, getting burned or drowning. There's nothing instinctive about the fear of escaping from the cocaine trap.

YOU HAVE NOTHING TO FEAR

Once you're free of the cocaine trap, you'll be amazed at how easy it was to escape. You'll find that you're able to derive far more pleasure from life, and your only regret will be not having made your escape sooner. Right now you might still feel like someone struggling to get out of a deep pit, but once you do get out, you'll realize your fears were groundless.

In order to achieve this success, you need to clear your mind of all doubt. Understand and accept that your fears of trying to live without cocaine are based on illusions. In reality, you have nothing to fear.

On the subject of falling back into the trap, some people ask, "How can you know for sure that something won't happen?" In other words, even if you do manage to quit cocaine, how do you know you won't fall into the trap again? After all, the chances of being struck by a meteorite are infinitesimally small, but nobody can say with absolute certainty that it will never happen to them.

That's very true; however, you have a considerable advantage over potential meteorite victims. If a meteorite is going to hit you, there's nothing you can do about it, whereas only you can make yourself go back to cocaine. You control that decision, and once you've seen through the con that lured you into the trap in the first place, you will have no difficulty in deciding to stay free.

If you still have doubts and fears at this stage, don't worry. That's not at all unusual. You've been brainwashed into thinking you have to go through some painful ordeal and make huge sacrifices to become a non-coke addict, and that even if you do succeed, you will be forever tempted to use cocaine.

This is not the case, and recognizing this fact is purely a matter of changing the way you look at the situation. Once you're in the right frame of mind, you will change your perception and the fear will leave.

The fifth instruction was to keep an open mind. If you have followed this instruction, you will have seen through the illusions to the true picture: that cocaine does absolutely nothing for you whatsoever. It's neither a source of pleasure nor support; in fact, it takes away genuine pleasures and leaves you feeling insecure.

If you are still unclear about this point, go back and read Chapter 3 again, making sure you allow your mind to take it all in. Relax, let go of your preconceptions, and allow the true picture to take shape in your mind. The key to seeing through any illusion is not willpower; it's letting go of your existing perceptions and allowing your mind to see it another way.

Chapter 13

FIRST STEPS TO FREEDOM

You've already come a long way in the process of unraveling the brainwashing that has kept you hooked on cocaine, and putting yourself in the right frame of mind to escape. Now you're going to start taking the practical forward steps that will help you become a happy non-coke addict for the rest of your life.

Your first positive step was choosing to read this book. You had a choice: you could have continued to bury your head in the sand and stumble further and further into the miserable slavery of cocaine addiction. Instead, you decided to take a positive action in order to resolve the situation. All you need to do is continue to make positive choices.

As we move forward, there are three very important facts that you need to remember:

1. COCAINE DOES ABSOLUTELY NOTHING FOR YOU AT ALL.

It's crucial that you understand why this is so, and accept it to be the case, so that you never get a feeling of deprivation or sacrifice.

2. THERE IS NO NEED FOR A TRANSITIONAL PERIOD.

With drug addicts, this is often referred to as the "withdrawal period." But anyone who quits with Easyway has no need to worry about the withdrawal period. Yes, it might take time to repair the physical damage caused by cocaine. But the moment you stop taking it is the moment you become free. You don't have to wait for anything to happen.

3. THERE IS NO SUCH THING AS "JUST ONE."

Just one line is enough to make you a cocaine addict, and must be seen for what it is: part of a lifelong chain of self-destruction. People who see that there is no benefit to using cocaine have no desire to do so, not even "just one."

KILL THE BIG MONSTER

Many addicts suffer from the illusion that they can never break free completely. They convince themselves that their addiction is their friend, their confidence, their support, even part of their identity. They fear that if they quit, they will not only lose their closest companion, they will lose a part of themselves. It's a stark indication of just how severely the brainwashing distorts our perceptions, that anyone should come to regard as a friend something that is destroying them and making them miserable.

When you lose a friend, you grieve. Eventually you come to terms with the loss, and life goes on; but you might be left with a genuine void in your life that you can never fill. There's nothing you can do about it. You have no choice but to accept the situation and, although it still hurts, you do.

When cocaine addicts and other addicts try to quit by using willpower, they feel they're losing a friend. They know they're making the right decision to stop, but they still suffer from a feeling of sacrifice and, therefore, there's a void in their lives. It isn't a genuine void, but they believe it is, so the effect is the same. They feel as if they're mourning for a friend.

But this false friend isn't even dead. The purveyors of these drugs make absolutely sure that their victims are forever subjected to the temptation of forbidden fruit for the rest of their lives.

When you rid yourself of your mortal enemy, there is no need to mourn. On the contrary, you can rejoice and celebrate from the start, and you can continue to rejoice and celebrate for the rest of your life.

GET IT CLEAR IN YOUR MIND THAT COCAINE IS NOT YOUR FRIEND.

Nor is it part of your identity. It never has been. In fact, it's your mortal enemy, and by getting rid of it you're sacrificing nothing—just making wonderful, positive gains.

So the answer to the question "When will I be free?" is "Whenever you choose to be." You could spend the next few days, and possibly the rest of your life, continuing to believe that cocaine was your friend and wondering when you'll stop missing it. If so, you'll feel miserable, the desire to use cocaine might never leave you, and you'll end up either feeling deprived for the rest of your life or going back to cocaine and feeling even worse.

Alternatively, you can recognize cocaine for the mortal enemy that it really is, and take pleasure in cutting it out of your life. Then you need never crave it again, and whenever it enters your mind you'll feel elated that it's no longer destroying you.

Unlike people who quit with the willpower method, you'll be happy to think about your old enemy, and you don't need to try to block it from your mind. On the contrary, enjoy thinking about it and rejoice that it no longer plagues your life.

KILL THE LITTLE MONSTER

We asked you to approach this process with a relaxed, rational and open mind, because that helps you understand the cocaine trap and the Little Monster that complains when you don't satisfy your urge to use coke. During the first few days after your final line, the Little Monster might be grumbling away, sending messages to your brain that it wants you to interpret as "I want a line."

But you now understand the true picture and, instead of using coke, or getting into a panic because you can't, pause for a moment. Take a deep breath. Remind yourself that there is nothing to fear. There is no pain. The feeling isn't bad. It's just the slight uncomfortable feeling that occurs when cocaine leaves your system. It's what coke addicts suffer throughout their addicted lives.

In the past, your mind interpreted the pangs of the Little Monster as "I want a line" because it had every reason to believe that cocaine would satisfy the empty, insecure feeling. But now, having killed the Big Monster, you understand that, far from relieving that feeling, it's cocaine that caused it.

So just relax, accept the feeling for what it really is—the death throes of the Little Monster—and remind yourself, "Non-coke addicts don't have this problem. This is a feeling that addicts suffer from, and they suffer from it throughout their cocaine-addicted lives. Isn't it great?! It will soon be gone forever." The withdrawal pangs will cease to feel like pangs and will become moments of pleasure.

During the first few days in particular, you might find that you forget you've quit. It can happen any time. You think, "I'll have a bump," and then you remember with joy that you're now a non-coke addict. But you wonder why the thought entered your head when you were convinced you'd reversed the brainwashing. Such times can be crucial in whether you succeed. React in the wrong way and they can be disastrous. Doubts can surface, and you might start to question your decision to quit and lose faith in yourself.

These occurrences won't come as a surprise if you're prepared for them. Have your mindset ready so that when they occur, you remain calm and use them as a reminder of the wonderful freedom you've gained. Instead of thinking, "I can't do this," you will think, "Isn't it great?! I don't need to use cocaine any more. I'm free!"

The associations you had with using cocaine, such as seeing friends, eating out, going to parties, etc, can linger after the Little Monster has died. For coke addicts who quit with the willpower method, this can seriously undermine their efforts. In their minds, they have built a powerful case against cocaine, they've decided to become a non-addict, they've managed to go for however long without the drug, but on certain occasions a voice keeps saying, "I want a line."

They haven't killed the Big Monster, so they still think of coke as a pleasure or support.

Although you will no longer suffer from the illusion that you're being deprived, it's still imperative that you prepare yourself for these situations. Occasionally forgetting that you no longer use cocaine isn't a bad sign, it's a very good one. It's proof that your life is returning to the happy state you were in before you got hooked on cocaine, when your whole existence wasn't dominated by a poisonous and highly addictive drug.

Remember the parking space analogy. Thoughts don't matter—it's what you do with the thoughts that matters.

Expecting these moments to happen and being prepared for them means you won't be caught off guard. You'll be wearing a suit of impregnable armor. You know you've made the correct decision, and nobody will be able to make you doubt it. Instead of being the cause of your downfall, these moments will give you added strength and pleasure, reminding you just how wonderful it is to be FREE!

THROW OFF THE BAGGAGE OF COKE ADDICTION

Everything you have read so far was designed to help you see the trap that you're in and recognize that you hold the key. The trap is the addiction. The key is unraveling the brainwashing that keeps you addicted—killing the Big Monster. The final step is to turn the key—to kill the Little Monster—and walk free.

By now, you should have a clear understanding of the cocaine trap and how it keeps you hooked by creating the illusion of pleasure. You should be completely clear that any benefit you thought you got from cocaine was merely an illusion created by a combination of the Little and Big Monsters.

You should be in no doubt that coke provides neither pleasure nor support. It does not give you courage. It does not make you more interesting or entertaining, nor does it help you get up for a night out. It's not a reward, it's pure punishment—a highly addictive poison that destroys you physically and mentally.

You should also be clear that the only way to control cocaine consumption is not to take it.

Cutting down or just having "the occasional line" is not the best of both worlds, it's the worst of both worlds. As long as you put cocaine in your system, it will control you. The only people who are not controlled by cocaine are people who don't take it: non-addicts.

You become a non-addict the moment you stop using coke without any desire to ever take it again. At that moment, the Little Monster will begin to die. This is nothing to fear. On the contrary, you should rejoice in its death throes. Remember, it's your mortal enemy and it's leaving you for good.

The fear that has prevented you from escaping from the cocaine trap before now is the fear that you won't be able to enjoy or deal with life without cocaine. Non-coke addicts don't have this fear. Cocaine doesn't relieve the fear, it causes it. It's fantastic to be free of this fear.

A major cause of stress for coke addicts is the effort they go to to keep their problem secret. It's much easier to overcome any problem if you're open and honest about it. But perhaps you find the idea of owning up unthinkable. You're afraid that your family and friends will be angry and will lose respect for you. It is possible that this will be the case. The people who love and trust you will be hurt, but in the end they will respect you for coming clean, and will want to help.

But it's more likely that the people you think you've been deceiving haven't been deceived at all. They've probably noticed the change in your behavior. They've probably been hurt by your irritability and brash behavior. They've probably become suspicious of your inability to apply yourself to work and other commitments. The longer you keep trying to deceive them, the more these feelings will grow into distrust and alienation. Come clean, and you give them a chance to understand why your behavior has changed, and to help you work on it.

Don't be surprised to find that they're relieved by your admission. You might feel that your loved ones are not ready for the full story of your cocaine addiction and that "dumping it on them" would be unfair. That's fine. You're the best person to judge when the time is right to share the truth. Once you're enjoying the confidence and self-respect that comes with your newfound freedom, you will be better equipped to figure out the best way to come clean... if that's what you'd like to do.

When you find that you're enjoying life and dealing with stress better as a non-coke addict, you will no longer have to try to block your mind to the terrible effects it had on you both physically and mentally. One of the huge bonuses of quitting is that you will no longer need to worry about them.

It's time to kill the Little Monster and escape from the cocaine trap. Remember, fear is not relieved by cocaine, it is caused by it. You have nothing to fear by stopping, only wonderful gains to make. Think about the fly on the funnel of the pitcher plant. You could set it free by encouraging it to fly out while it still has a chance.

Remember, cocaine does absolutely nothing for you whatsoever. It's a poison that causes immense damage to the length and quality of your life. You can stop the damage immediately by never using cocaine again. You have nothing to lose and everything to gain.

What do you think when you see a heroin addict? Isn't it obvious that each time they inject the drug into a vein they're not curing their problem but making it worse, and that the only thing that will end the problem for them is to stop taking heroin?

Think about the ex-con who's in danger of jeopardizing his freedom by reoffending, because he's afraid of life outside prison. Put yourself in his position. Remind him of all the wonderful advantages there are to being free. Remind yourself of all the wonderful gains you will make without cocaine in your life.

- Better health
- Fewer mood swings
- Better relationships
- Higher self-esteem
- Less stress

- Better sleep
- Concentration
- Clearer thinking
- More money
- More time

This is your chance to fly free. In fact, you can fly free any time you choose, so why wait? You have nothing to fear. Remember, awful things are guaranteed to happen as long as you stay in the cocaine trap. Escape and you can take control of putting your life back together.

You will be amazed by how good it feels to be free of the slavery of cocaine addiction.

Chapter 14

READY TO QUIT

Very soon you'll be asked to make a solemn vow that you will never use cocaine, or anything similar to it, again.

When you've finished your final line, you might be aware of the withdrawal for a few days. Remember, this is not a physical pain; it's just the faint cries of the Little Monster wanting to be fed.

However, as faint as it is, you should not ignore it. It's essential to keep in mind the fact that the Little Monster was created when you first started using coke, and it has continued to feed on every subsequent line you've had.

As soon as you stop using coke, you cut off the supply to the Little Monster and it begins to die. In its death throes, it will try to get you to feed it. Create a mental image of this parasite getting weaker and weaker, and enjoy starving it to death. Keep this mental image with you at all times and make sure you don't respond to its death throes by thinking, "I need a line."

Remember that the empty, insecure feeling was caused by your last bump of cocaine. The feeling itself isn't pleasurable, but you will enjoy it because you will understand the cause and know that the Little Monster inside you is dying.

Take delight in killing off the Little Monster. Even if you do get that feeling of "I want a line" for a few days, don't worry about it. Remember, it's not a line you want; it's relief from that nagging feeling, which will go away permanently as long as you never use cocaine again.

If you were to have a line, it would guarantee you suffer from it for the rest of your life. It's just the Little Monster doing everything it can to tempt you to feed it. As long as you see that, you will find it easy to starve it to death. You now have complete control over it. It's no longer destroying you; you're destroying it, and soon you will be free forever. Noticing the Little Monster as it dies will make you smile and feel invincible, not bother you.

NO NEED TO WAIT

The good news is that you can start enjoying the genuine pleasure of being a non-coke addict from the moment you finish your final line. Unlike the willpower method, with Easyway you don't have to wait for anything.

It takes just a few days for the physical withdrawal to pass. During this time, people who use willpower tend to feel completely obsessed with being denied what they see as their pleasure or support. Then, after about three weeks, there might come a time when they suddenly realize that they have not thought about cocaine for a while. It's an exciting feeling... and a dangerous moment.

They've gone from believing that life will always be miserable without being able to use cocaine, to believing that time will solve their problem. They feel great—surely this is the cure. It's time to celebrate. What possible harm could it do to reward themselves with just one line?

Clearly the Big Monster is still alive. They still believe that they've been denying themselves some kind of pleasure. If they're stupid enough to have a line, they won't find it rewarding at all. It will give them no feeling of pleasure or support. The only reason they ever experienced the illusion of pleasure from cocaine is that it partially relieved the symptoms of withdrawal. But now that they're no longer withdrawing from cocaine, they will not even experience that illusion.

But that one line is enough to revive the Little Monster. Now panic starts to creep back in. They don't want their efforts to quit to be blown away so easily, and for nothing, so they draw on their willpower and try not to give in to the urge to have another line. But after a while the same thing happens. They regain their confidence and the temptation to have "just one" rears its ugly head again. This time they can say to themselves, "I did it last time and didn't get hooked, so what's the harm in doing it again?"

They're wandering back into the trap.

Does this ring any bells? Anyone who has tried to quit with the willpower method is likely to have experienced something similar. With Easyway, when you realize you haven't thought about cocaine for a while, your first thought is not to celebrate with a line, it's:

GREAT—I'M FREE!

There is no feeling of deprivation. You can relax from the moment you finish your final line, and rather than interpreting the feeling as "I want a line," you think, "Great! Isn't it wonderful? I don't ever have to go through that misery again."

Many ex-cocaine addicts who quit with the willpower method never get to the point where they can say that with certainty. They're never quite sure whether they've kicked it. The physical withdrawal symptoms feel like normal anxiety and stress, so when they experience these feelings they interpret them as "I want a line."

Of course, using cocaine at this stage wouldn't even give the illusion of relieving these natural pangs; they have no withdrawal, but they don't know that. They're still convinced that coke will help. The real stress is now increased, because they believe that they're being deprived of a support that will ease the situation.

They're faced with a dilemma: go through the rest of their life believing they're missing out, or find out for sure. Sadly, the only way to do that is to use coke again. If they do, they find that their stress is not relieved—in fact, it's increased by their sense of disappointment at having given in to temptation. But they've revived the Little Monster, and the outcome is that pretty soon they'll be using cocaine just like before.

In a little while, you'll have your final line and make a solemn vow never to use cocaine, or anything similar, again. If this thought makes you panic, remind yourself of these simple facts:

• THE DRUG INDUSTRY DEPENDS ON THAT PANIC TO KEEP YOU HOOKED.

Have you ever thought about the havoc, the misery, the violence, the suffering that the cocaine industry inflicts across the world? We close our mind to it because it upsets us to think that we are fueling all that crime and destruction. You don't need to turn your mind away from it anymore—you can feel fabulous to be free of it all.

• COCAINE DOESN'T RELIEVE THE PANIC, IT CAUSES IT.

Take a moment to compose yourself. Do you really have any reason to panic? Nothing bad is going to happen as a result of you quitting cocaine. You have only wonderful gains to make. Perhaps you're afraid of going into unknown territory. There is nothing unknown about what you're about to do. It's something you've already done thousands of times before, every time you've snorted your last line at the end of the evening. This particular line will be a very, very special one. It will be your last.

If you stopped using cocaine before you started this book, that's fine, as long as you're confident that you have killed the Big Monster and you have no doubts whatsoever that you're not making a sacrifice or depriving yourself in any way. You don't need to have a final line—just confirm to yourself that you've already had one, and then make the vow.

Very soon you will feel stronger, both physically and mentally. You will have more energy, more confidence, more self-respect, and more money. It's essential that you don't put off this wonderful freedom, not for a week, a day, or a second. Waiting for something to happen is one of the reasons why cocaine addicts using the willpower method find it so difficult.

What are they waiting for? To find out if they'll ever use cocaine again? There's only one way to find that out...

So instead they're just left waiting, waiting, for the rest of their lives.

You become a non-cocaine addict the moment you finish your final line and make the vow.

What you're achieving is a new frame of mind, an understanding that cocaine does nothing for you and that by not using coke you're freeing yourself from a life of slavery, misery, and degradation.

Replace any panic you might have felt with a feeling of excitement. You no longer need to be sick, incapable, secretive, or dishonest. You're about to discover the joy of taking control.

REJOICE!

This is going to be one of the best experiences you've ever had.

YOU'RE ABOUT TO BECOME FREE!

FINAL CHECKS

It's time for some final checks before you make your leap to freedom.

Earlier we compared the feeling of freedom when you escape the cocaine trap to the exhilaration of a parachute jump. What you're about to do will be one of the most exciting experiences of your life, so let's make sure that everything goes according to plan, and run through a final checklist to make sure you're prepared.

Your frame of mind should be, "Great! I don't need cocaine any more. I'm about to free myself from a prison of misery and degradation. I can't wait!"

You have every reason to celebrate. You're about to walk free of an evil trap, which has kept you imprisoned and severely disrupted your life, making you miserable, confused, scared and angry. You're about to regain control over your life and banish those feelings of slavery and powerlessness for good. Very soon you will be a non-coke addict.

Take pride in your achievement; there are millions of cocaine addicts in the world who wish they could be in your shoes. Soon you will rediscover the unbridled joy of feeling healthy, having nothing to hide, and having time for the people you love and the things you love to do.

While you were in the cocaine trap, you forgot how to enjoy the genuine pleasures in life. You're about to get that huge part of your life back.

WHAT YOU NOW KNOW

We have unraveled the brainwashing and dispelled the illusions that made you believe that cocaine gave you pleasure and support. You know and understand that cocaine is an addictive poison that will eventually destroy you, physically and mentally.

You have seen through the myths that kept you in the cocaine trap. You know that coke doesn't relieve stress and anxiety, it causes them; it's not a social lubricant, it's a social saboteur; it doesn't give you courage, it undermines it; and it doesn't help you think, it impairs judgment.

The reason why you haven't been able to stop using cocaine in the past is not because there's something wonderful about it that you can't live without, nor is it a flaw in your personality. It's because you followed the wrong method.

Now you understand that coke gives you neither pleasure nor support, and the only reason you ever thought it did was because each line brought a little bit of relief from the craving caused by the line before. You have been addicted to a drug that takes control away from you, but still tricks you into thinking you're in control. You have accepted that cocaine made you a slave, and the only way to escape that slavery is to stop.

READY TO STOP

As you prepare to take your final line and quit cocaine for good, you should be in no doubt that the decision you're making isn't just the right one, it's the only one if you don't want to spend the rest of your life as a slave to cocaine.

You understand that any lingering pangs after you stop are just the cries of the Little Monster as it takes its last breath. Enjoy the feeling—it's the feeling of freedom. Nothing can distract you now.

Very soon you will undertake the ritual of your final line. As I've said, if you've already had your final line, that's fine—you don't need to do another one. Just confirm to yourself that you've had your final line.

If you haven't had your final line, you might be wondering when the ideal moment would be to do it.

THE PERFECT TIME TO QUIT

There are two typical occasions that tend to trigger attempts to quit, whether it's cocaine, smoking, gambling or anything else that is disrupting your life. One is a traumatic event, such as a health scare or a financial blow, the other is a "special" day, such as a birthday or New Year's Day.

I call these "meaningless days," because they actually have no bearing whatsoever on your addiction, other than providing a target date for you to make your attempt to stop. That would be fine if it helped, but meaningless days actually cause more harm than good.

New Year's Day is the most popular of all meaningless days, a clear marker of the end of one period and the beginning of another. It also happens to have the lowest success rate. The holiday season is when we party more than usual, and by New Year's Eve we're just about ready for a break. So we have one last binge and then, as the clock strikes midnight, we vow that we'll quit.

We very quickly start to feel cleansed, but the Little Monster is demanding its fix. If we're using the wrong method, we interpret these cries as "I want a line," and although we might hold out to begin with, eventually the Big Monster will have its way and we'll find ourselves back in the trap. Meaningless days just encourage us to go through the damaging cycle of half-hearted attempts to quit, bringing on the feeling of deprivation, followed by the sense of failure that reinforces the illusion that stopping is difficult and might be impossible. Cocaine addicts spend their lives looking for excuses to put off "the dreaded day." Meaningless days provide the perfect excuse to say, "I will quit—just not today."

Having said that: if you're reading this on a meaningless day, don't worry—with Easyway you will be successful regardless of the date, not because of it.

When trauma strikes, you respond by saying it's time to get your act together. But these stressful times are also when your desire to use cocaine becomes strongest, because you regard cocaine as a form of support. This is another ingenuity of the trap.

Some coke addicts choose their annual vacation, thinking they'll be able to cope better if they're away from the everyday stresses of work and home life, and the usual temptations to use coke. Others pick a time when there are no social events coming up where they will find it difficult not to use coke. These approaches might work for a while, but they leave a lingering doubt: "OK, I've coped so far, but what about when I go back to work, or that big party happens?"

When you quit with Easyway, we encourage you to go out and handle stress, and throw yourself into social events right away, so that you can prove to yourself from the start that, even at times when you feared you would find it hard to cope without cocaine, you're still happy to be free.

If you saw someone you love hurting themselves repeatedly, what would you say? Would you ask them to stop the next time a convenient moment arises? Or would you ask them to stop right away?

DO IT NOW!

That's what the people who love you would say if they knew about your cocaine problem. You have everything you need to quit. Like an athlete on the blocks at the start of the race, you're in peak condition to ensure success.

LOOK FORWARD TO GETTING YOUR (REAL) LIFE BACK

Think of everything you have to gain: a life free of slavery, dishonesty, misery, anger, deceit, self-loathing, impotence. No more scratching around for money; no more lying to people about what you need it for; no more hiding yourself away or trying to cover your tracks; no more feeling disappointed, guilty and weak.

In place of all that misery, you can look forward to living in the light, with your head held high, enjoying open, honest relationships with the people around you, feeling in control of how you spend your time and money, and finding joy in the genuine pleasures you enjoyed before you walked into the cocaine trap.

With so much happiness to gain and so much misery to rid yourself of, what possible reason is there to wait? It's time for the seventh instruction:

MAKE A SOLEMN VOW NEVER TO USE COCAINE, OR ANYTHING LIKE IT, AGAIN.

The vow marks the breaking point in the cycle of addiction. It's important that you observe this ritual, because as soon as you complete it, you're free.

The time has come. You're about to escape from one of the most subtle and insidious traps ever devised. All along we've promised you it would be easy, but that shouldn't diminish your sense of achievement in any way. To go through the method as instructed, and understand the nature of the trap, requires considerable discipline and perseverance. It also takes courage to open your mind.

Be proud of your achievement. You've reached a position that millions of cocaine addicts wish they could achieve. If you feel nervous, don't worry about it. That's completely normal at this stage, and is no threat to your chances of success. When you make a parachute jump, the last-minute nerves quickly turn to exhilaration as your parachute opens and you realize that everything you've learned and prepared for is working exactly how they told you it would.

It's impossible to put into words the utter joy of the person who has finally accepted that they don't need to use coke any more. The elation is unbelievable. It's like a huge, dark shadow being removed from your mind. You no longer need to despise yourself, or worry about what it's been doing to your health, or all the money you waste.

You no longer have to worry about where the next line is coming from. You'll no longer feel weak, miserable, sordid, incomplete, or guilty.

You're in that position now, standing by the plane door, ready to jump. You have all the knowledge and understanding you need to make this the best experience of your life. Soon you will be flying free. You have nothing to fear.

The only thing that is facing sudden death is your cocaine problem. You are not losing a friend; you have no reason to grieve. On the contrary, you should rejoice in the destruction of your mortal enemy.

Remind yourself that you're not "giving up" anything. You had no need to use cocaine before you started; you have no need to use cocaine now. Lifelong non-coke addicts and ex-coke addicts are very happy without cocaine in their lives.

What pleasure does it give? What support does it provide? If you've followed and understood everything up to this point, you will have come to the obvious conclusion:

COCAINE DOES NOTHING FOR YOU WHATSOEVER.

Chapter 15

YOUR FINAL LINE

Very soon you'll be asked to take your final line, or confirm that you've done so, and make your solemn vow never to use cocaine again. Before you do, it's essential that you're completely reconciled with the notion of never using coke again.

You must be absolutely clear that cocaine gives you no pleasure or support whatsoever, and you're not making any sort of sacrifice. If you find the thought of never having coke again difficult to accept, try taking on board the only alternative: a lifetime of slavery and misery.

It's a simple choice. If you still feel as if you're being made to choose the lesser of two evils, ask yourself this: does it concern you that you might never suffer from the flu again, or that you might never have a heart attack, or that you might never inject yourself with heroin?

No? Then why should it bother you that you will never again suffer at the hands of one of the world's worst drugs? Cocaine.

Cocaine addiction is a disease. It started when you began to consume the addictive poison. It ends when you finish your final line and make your vow.

It's ridiculously easy to stop using cocaine as long as you understand that there's nothing to give up, and you follow all the instructions. You're stopping because you detest being a slave to coke, so instead of thinking, "I must never use cocaine again," start thinking,

"GREAT! I NO LONGER HAVE TO WASTE MY TIME AND MONEY MAKING MYSELF MISERABLE AGAIN. I'M FREE!"

This is a momentous occasion, and one of the most important decisions you'll ever make. You're freeing yourself from slavery and achieving something wonderful, something all cocaine addicts would love to achieve and something that everybody, coke addicts and non-coke addicts alike, will admire and respect you for. What's more, you'll rise in the estimation of one person in particular:

YOU!

You should now be feeling excited about finally ending the misery that cocaine has caused you. If you've already stopped, do not do another line now, just confirm to yourself that you've had your final dose of cocaine.

The thing that makes it difficult to quit is not the physical aggravation of withdrawal, it's the doubt, the uncertainty, the waiting to become a non-coke addict. With this method, you become a non-addict the moment you finish your final line and make your vow never to use cocaine, or anything like it, again.

It's important to know when that moment is, to be able to make that vow with a feeling of venom, to visualize your triumph over the Little Monster and be able to say,

"YES! I'M A NON-COCAINE ADDICT NOW. I'M FREE!"

Your mindset at this moment should be one of certainty. It's not enough to hope that you will never use cocaine again; you need to know. But don't worry if you feel apprehensive and nervous—there really isn't a right way or a wrong way to feel. So let's just go over the things that might cause you to doubt your decision. Get it clearly into your mind:

THERE IS ABSOLUTELY NOTHING TO GIVE UP.

Cocaine gives no genuine pleasure or support whatsoever. The fact that it appears to is just an illusion. You understand how that illusion is created by using cocaine in the first place, and that quitting is easy if you remember this one fact:

THERE IS ONLY ONE ESSENTIAL TO BEING A NON-COCAINE ADDICT AND THAT IS NOT TO USE COCAINE—EVER.

In order to be a happy non-cocaine addict for life, it's essential that you never desire to use cocaine. If you have a desire to have just one bump, or line, you'll have a desire to have another and another.

Get it clearly into your mind: it has to be all or nothing.

There are two other factors that can make you doubt your decision:

1. THE BELIEF THAT YOU HAVE AN ADDICTIVE PERSONALITY

Anyone can fall for the cocaine trap—and many people do. Even if you did have an addictive personality, that would simply mean that you easily get addicted, it would not mean that you would find it difficult to stop.

2. OTHER COKE ADDICTS

They're the ones who are losing out, not you. Having read this book, you have infinitely more expertise on the subject than they have. Don't envy them, pity them. They're still in the trap; you are escaping.

You are about to make the decision to have your final line and vow never to consume cocaine again. If you made that decision before you elected to read this book, you just need to reconfirm the decision in your mind now. This is the moment when you walk free.

Think about the misery and suffering that cocaine has caused you. Visualize the Little Monster and how it has dominated your life. Imagine it laughing at you. This is the time for your revenge. Make your vow. No more slavery! No more misery! You're cutting off its lifeline and destroying that evil tyrant once and for all.

I WOULD NOW LIKE YOU TO TAKE YOUR FINAL LINE/SHOT OF COCAINE

Now is the time to do your final line.

Now pause and think about what you've achieved.

You will never have to do it again.

REJOICE! YOU'RE FREE!

Now make a promise, a commitment, a solemn vow, to yourself, that you will never use cocaine, or anything similar, again.

SEAL YOUR VICTORY

Revel in your victory. This is one of the greatest achievements of your life. It's important that this moment sticks in your mind. Be aware that, at this moment, you're fired up with powerful reasons to stop. But as the days, weeks, and years slip by, your memory of how you were feeling about cocaine today might fade. Implant those thoughts in your mind now, while they're vivid, so that even if your memory of the details should diminish, your resolution never to use cocaine again does not.

If you're prepared for a challenge, it doesn't faze you the way it would if it took you by surprise. You can easily deal with any moments of doubt in the future by having the foresight to plan ahead.

In a few months, you'll find it difficult to believe that you once found it necessary to use cocaine, let alone how it controlled your life. You might also lose your fear of getting hooked again. Be aware now, in advance, that this can be a danger; you might have moments when you're on a complete natural high, surrounded by people using cocaine, or you might experience a trauma and your guard will be down. Anticipate these situations now and make it part of your vow that, if and when they come, you will be prepared, so there's no way you'll be led into starting to use cocaine again.

Keep it clearly in your mind that cocaine neither made the good times better nor relieved stress during the bad times. It did the complete opposite.

Now you can move on. Don't wait for anything. Embrace this moment with a feeling of excitement and elation.

THE NIGHTMARE IS OVER.

Chapter 16

FREEDOM STARTS HERE

Congratulations! You're now a non-cocaine addict and will remain one permanently, as long as you never doubt your decision. You became a non-coke addict the moment you finished your final line. You can immediately go on with your life and enjoy the many pleasures it has to offer.

For a few days, you might detect the cries of the Little Monster as it goes through its death throes. This is nothing to worry about, so don't try to block it from your mind. Recognize the cries and rejoice in what they signify—the death of the monster that has held you enslaved all this time.

As a coke addict, you felt compelled to feed the Little Monster. Now that you're free, you don't have to do anything. Killing the Little Monster is easy:

DO NOTHING!

Except smile, of course.

Prepare your mind so you're ready with the right response in the event that you feel the Little Monster dying. Instead of thinking, "I want a line, but I'm not allowed one," think, "This is the Little Monster demanding its fix. This is what coke addicts suffer from throughout their addicted lives. Non-coke addicts don't suffer from this feeling. Isn't it great?! I'm a non-cocaine addict, and I'm free!"

Remind yourself that there is no physical pain, and that the only discomfort you might be feeling is not because you've stopped using coke but because you started in the first place. Also be clear that having another line, far from relieving that discomfort, would ensure that you suffer for the rest of your life.

Prepare your mind to respond in this way, and any withdrawal pangs will become moments of pleasure. Revel in the Little Monster's death throes. Feel no guilt about rejoicing in its death; after all, it's been killing you, making you miserable, and keeping you a slave long enough.

People trying to quit with the willpower method are forever moping about something they hope they'll never do, forever waiting for nothing to happen. But when you have no desire to use cocaine, you don't have to wait or mope about anything. You don't have to stand by and grit your teeth while the Little Monster dies; you can move on and enjoy life as a non-coke addict.

One of the fantastic benefits of becoming free of cocaine is that you rediscover the joy of life's genuine pleasures. When you're addicted to coke, you lose the ability fully to enjoy things that non-coke addicts enjoy most: reading books, going out, being entertained, attending social events, getting exercise, having better sex… Now that you're free of cocaine, you have all these pleasures to get excited about again.

You will find that situations you once regarded as unstimulating or even irritating are becoming enjoyable again: things like spending time with loved ones and going for walks. Work will become more enjoyable as you discover that you're better able to concentrate, think creatively, and handle stress.

CHOOSE YOUR PLEASURES

At the same time, you become more discerning about the things you don't like. Most people suddenly realize when they stop using cocaine that they've wasted a lot of time going to boring events that gave them no pleasure at all.

They would use cocaine, thinking it would help them relax, or enjoy the boring occasion or event. But when they stop using coke, they can see that it wasn't their fault those occasions seemed boring—they *were* boring.

Deciding to stop doing things you find dull and boring is incredibly empowering. When you cut cocaine out of your life, you regain the ability to see things as they really are, and make better decisions about how you run your life.

DIFFICULT DAYS HAPPEN TO EVERYONE

Be prepared for bad days that are entirely unrelated to the fact that you've gotten cocaine out of your life. Everybody, coke addict and non-coke addict alike, has days when everything that can go wrong seems to. It has nothing to do with the fact that you've stopped using cocaine.

The truth is, when you stop using coke you find that the bad days don't come around as frequently; and when they do, you feel stronger and can deal with them.

You might find that when you have bad days, or even very good days, the thought of using coke enters your mind. That's not unusual, and it's nothing to worry about. You don't have to push the thought out of your mind. You just have to recognize it for what it is: a remnant from the days when you responded to every setback or celebration by using cocaine.

It doesn't mean you're still vulnerable to the trap—it just means you're still adjusting to your newfound freedom. Rather than thinking, "I mustn't use coke," or, "I thought I'd overcome this addiction," think, "Great! I don't have to use cocaine any more. I'm free!"

The thought will pass very quickly, and your brain will soon adjust.

There are just a few final instructions. The eighth instruction is clear:

NEVER DOUBT YOUR DECISION TO QUIT.

This is essential. Never make the mistake that people who use the willpower method make, of craving another line. If you do, you will put yourself in the same impossible position they are in: miserable if you don't and even more miserable if you do.

If you were asked, "Do you want to be a cocaine addict for the rest of your life?" your answer would be, "No way!" Nothing will ever change your answer to that question. So never be fooled into thinking in terms of one line, or a few lines. See the reality: a lifelong chain of filth, misery, and disease. And you've escaped.

The ninth instruction is:

IGNORE ANYTHING YOU READ ABOUT COCAINE, OR HEAR ABOUT COCAINE, THAT CONFLICTS WITH EASYWAY.

Be skeptical of anything that contradicts what you've learned in this program and you'll be happily immune to it.

The tenth and final instruction is one that you have already decided for yourself:

NEVER USE COCAINE AGAIN.

Also never forget that if you ever have any uncertainties or concerns about cocaine, or a question arises in your mind, or you just have a nagging doubt about your freedom—everyone at Easyway is here for you. We answer thousands of questions a year, and never tire of doing so... supporting former addicts in their enjoyment of their freedom makes us incredibly happy—so please don't hesitate to get in touch. All that's left for me to say is CONGRATULATIONS on being free, and all the best for your future:

FREE OF COCAINE!

ALLEN CARR'S EASYWAY CENTERS

The following list indicates the countries where Allen Carr's Easyway To Stop Smoking Centers are currently operational.

Check www.allencarr.com for latest additions to this list.

The success rate at the centers, based on the three-month money-back guarantee, is over 90 per cent.

Selected centers also offer sessions that deal with alcohol, other drugs and weight issues. Please check with your nearest centre, listed below, for details.

Allen Carr's Easyway guarantees that you will find it easy to stop at the centers or your money back.

JOIN US!

Allen Carr's Easyway Centers have spread throughout the world with incredible speed and success. Our global franchise network now covers more than 150 cities in over 50 countries. This amazing growth has been achieved entirely organically. Former addicts, just like you, were so impressed by the ease with which they stopped that they felt inspired to contact us to see how they could bring the method to their region.

If you feel the same, contact us for details on how to become an Allen Carr's Easyway To Stop Smoking or an Allen Carr's Easyway To Stop Drinking franchisee.

Email us at: join-us@allencarr.com including your full name, postal address and region of interest.

SUPPORT US!

No, don't send us money!

You have achieved something really marvellous. Every time we hear of someone escaping from the sinking ship, we get a feeling of enormous satisfaction.

It would give us great pleasure to hear that you have freed yourself from the slavery of addiction, so please visit the following web page where you can tell us of your success, inspire others to follow in your footsteps and hear about ways you can help to spread the word.

 www.allencarr.com/fanzone

You can "like" our Facebook page here **www.facebook.com/AllenCarr**

Together, we can help further Allen Carr's mission: to cure the world of addiction.

CENTERS

Allen Carr's Easyway
Worldwide Head Office
Park House, 14 Pepys Road, Raynes Park
London SW20 8NH
Tel: +44 (0) 208 944 7761
Email: mail@allencarr.com
Website: www.allencarr.com

Worldwide Press Office
Tel: +44 (0) 7970 88 44 52
Email: Media@allencarr.com

USA Toll Free Booking Line
855 440 3777
Email: support@usa.allencarr.com

Australia	Netherlands
Austria	New Zealand
Belgium	Norway
Brazil	Peru
Bulgaria	Poland
Canada	Portugal
Chile	Republic of Ireland
Cyprus	Romania
Denmark	Russia
Estonia	Saudi Arabia
Finland	Serbia
France	Singapore
Germany	Slovenia
Greece	South Africa
Guatemala	South Korea
Hong Kong	Spain
Hungary	Sweden
India	Switzerland
Iran	Turkey
Israel	UAE
Italy	United Kingdom
Japan	USA
Lebanon	
Mauritius	
Mexico	

OTHER ALLEN CARR PUBLICATIONS

Allen Carr's revolutionary Easyway method is available in a wide variety of formats, including digitally as audiobooks and ebooks, and has been successfully applied to a broad range of subjects.

For more information about Easyway publications,
please visit **shop.allencarr.com**

Easyway to Quit Cannabis

Easyway to Quit Smoking

Stop Smoking Now

Quit Smoking Boot Camp

Your Personal Stop Smoking Plan

The Illustrated Easy Way to Stop Smoking

The Easy Way for Women to Stop Smoking

The Illustrated Easy Way for Women to Stop Smoking

Finally Free!

Smoking Sucks (Parent Guide with 16 page pull-out comic)

The Little Book of Quitting Smoking

How to Be a Happy Non-smoker

No More Ashtrays

How to Stop Your Child Smoking

The Only Way to Stop Smoking Permanently

Stop Drinking Now

The Easy Way to Control Alcohol

Your Personal Stop Drinking Plan

The Illustrated Easy Way to Stop Drinking

The Easy Way for Women to Stop Drinking

No More Hangovers

The Easy Way to Mindfulness

Good Sugar Bad Sugar

The Easy Way to Quit Sugar

Lose Weight Now

The Easy Way for Women to Lose Weight

No More Diets

The Easy Way to Lose Weight

The Easy Way to Stop Gambling

No More Gambling

No More Worrying

Get Out of Debt Now

No More Debt

No More Fear of Flying

The Easy Way to Quit Caffeine

Packing It In The Easy Way (the autobiography)

Want Easyway on your smartphone or tablet?
Search for "Allen Carr" in your app store.

Easyway publications are also available as audiobooks.
Visit shop.allencarr.com to find out more.

DISCOUNT COUPON
for
ALLEN CARR'S
EASYWAY CENTERS

Recover the price of this book when you attend an
Allen Carr's Easyway Center
anywhere in the world!

Allen Carr's Easyway has a global network of stop
smoking centers where we guarantee you'll find it easy
to stop smoking or your money back.

**The success rate based on this
unique money-back guarantee is over 90 per cent.**

Sessions addressing weight, alcohol and other
drug addictions are also available at certain centers.

When you book your session, mention this
coupon and you'll receive a discount of
the price of this book. Contact your nearest
center for more information on how the sessions
work and to book your appointment.

**Details of Allen Carr's Easyway
Centers can be found at**
www.allencarr.com

This offer is not valid in conjunction with any other offer/promotion.